<sup></sup>the
publishing
CIRCLE

978-1-955018-38-8 softcover
978-1-955018-39-5 large print
978-1-955018-40-1 hardcase
978-1-955018-41-8 eBook

# Contents

Contents

# About This Book

The creation of this book came about because of the huge need to provide people with food—a need present in every country on earth. I wanted to find a way to expand my donations and knew the best way to do that would be to have others join me. Using my skills as a publisher, I hoped to get others to contribute chapters so the knowledge would come from a collection of wisdom far beyond my own. I'd soon learn those who contributed came with willing hearts, plus amazing wisdom.

To make everything work well, it was essential to figure out what would be of value to readers. One thing I saw missing in the arena of books for female entrepreneurs was a comprehensive guide that included multiple perspectives, multiple approaches, and knowledge from women who were already successful.

Putting together a book that offered the perspective of women who didn't mimic the "get it right now or it's gone in the next five minutes" approach of some male entrepreneurs felt important, too. Thus the subtitle *The How-To Guide to Successful Entrepreneurship & Profiting In Business Without Sacrificing Integrity.*

I already knew several women who would be a good fit for the book. I pulled upon the power of those women and their connections to help flesh out the invitations to contribute chapters.

My dear friend Laura Steward was a huge help with the initial connections (and provided a lot of personal support), then

Christina Daves hopped in to make connections; Kendra Lee offered other names; Wendy Barr helped with some last-minute spots that needed to be filled; and Carla King made additional connections. Along the way, I met other women who loved the cause and wanted to help. Some men did, too, and you'll see two chapters written by them—men who have the same spirit of wanting to help others.

You'll see the topics and the personalities are diverse . . . exactly as they should be. As you go through the book, you'll find chapters that resonate and, perhaps, some that don't. What I believe you absolutely *will* find are some pieces that inspire you and/or prompt ideas.

Putting in this kind of effort without compensation for anyone (including me), meant there had to be benefits for everyone.

Those formed in this way:

**Benefits for you, the reader** – Knowledge, plus a gift from each of the authors. Those gifts range in value, but I think it's safe to say if you purchased everything offered, you'd be paying at least a couple of thousand dollars.

**Benefits to the contributors** – Increased visibility and, when anyone downloaded their gift, they would be able to communicate with that person in the future.

**Benefits to the charities** – The biggest amount will go to provide food for the hungry. As time passes, other charities may be included. No operational costs or my time or expenses are taken out, nor are any contributors paid, so you can feel confident the lion's share of your purchase will go to charity. Obviously, printing and shipping charges and the fees of distributors (such as Amazon) come out, but the bulk of the income goes to help those in need.

The benefits to me have come in the form of building relationships with wonderful people—people who, like me, want to make a difference in the world.

We can each play a role in making the world better. It's by combining the efforts of many that we bring about change.

Thank you for being a part of that change!

With love and blessings,

Linda Stirling

*"In all you do, BE the blessing."*
– LINDA STIRLING

# Introduction

## LINDA STIRLING

H ave you ever had someone laugh in your face when you told them you wanted to accomplish something?

I have.

In the mid-70s, I started work at a daily newspaper. My goal from the get-go was to be one of the writers there, but the only "in" was through a position selling advertising. At that time in my life, I hadn't acquired a college degree . . . in anything, much less journalism. As a single mom with three children under the age of six, the odds of being able to attend college anytime soon weren't good. Nevertheless, I was determined to be one of the newspaper's writers.

*Somehow, someway,* I told myself.

I knew that to be taken seriously I needed to first excel at the job I'd been hired to do. I put in the hours to make sure I consistently reached and exceeded the goals set by the advertising manager.

During my lunch hour or after work, I poured through the collection of newspapers from around the country. I hoped to find something in other newspapers that didn't exist in the newspaper where I worked. Day after day, week after week, I scoured everything I could get my hands on. At last, I realized there was one thing in common with other papers that the newspaper I worked for didn't have: a cohesive business section.

What got me even more excited was the fact that I knew the local businesses well because I was already selling them ads.

Logic told me that going to the publisher with just the idea of having a devoted business section wouldn't be enough to score me the position I craved. So, each evening after work, I paid the babysitter extra to stay late, or begged family members to watch the kids so I could work on my goal.

One evening, the department manager happened to be working late, too. She knew I'd finished everything required for the ad department, so she asked what I was doing. She'd always been friendly. Because of this, I didn't hesitate to share my dream.

"I'm working on a draft for a business page. I want to be the Business Editor for the paper," I told her.

She began to laugh, her laughter so loud it nearly drowned out the hum of the presses that could always be heard at that hour. When she finally caught her breath, she said, "You can't do that! You don't even have a college degree!" The laughter started in again.

I smiled and merely nodded before saying a quick good night and heading to my car, letting the tears stream down my face once inside that safe cocoon.

She was right. What was I thinking? If this was such a riotous thought to her, how would the publisher respond? I knew, too, there weren't any openings for reporters. The chances of succeeding seemed insurmountable.

I cried all the way home, forcing myself to finally settle down so my children wouldn't be affected.

When it came time for them to go to bed, I tucked them in and retreated to the couch. On autopilot from the months I'd spent planning, I went through my notebook of article ideas. The feeling of despair hit me again, and with it, an image of the department manager's face as she laughed at me.

No one had ever encouraged my dreams, but at least no one had laughed at them—until now.

I thought about my reason for wanting to write for the paper. At the forefront of reasons was that I wanted my children to be proud of me. I wanted to be proud of myself, too. There was the thought of making more money as well . . . money so I could do more for my family.

Looking at my reasons, I felt a different feeling rise within my core. My situation wouldn't be changing anytime soon, so I had to work with what I had or give up entirely. I asked myself this: How would I feel if someone told one of my children they couldn't do something? Told them they weren't smart enough or skilled enough? With that thought, I got my gumption back.

Over the next few days, I proceeded to finish a mockup of my plans. In newspaper language, two facing paces are called a double truck. I printed out examples of headlines and drew out my proposal as visually as I could. At the top of the first page, I put my name, along with the title, Business Editor.

I asked the publisher if I could schedule a meeting with him. On the day I was to meet him, my stomach roiled in fear, but I kept my resolve as I marched into his office with the portfolio cover that held my precious mockup.

Not easing into the topic, I blurted, "I want to be the Business Editor." Before he had a chance to say anything or, heaven forbid, laugh in my face like the manager had, I launched into my spiel.

I spoke about how other newspapers had devoted sections for business coverage and how I believed having one could benefit the community and tidy up the random coverage that currently existed. I spoke, too, about how I was the perfect person to do this because I already worked with the businesses and had the familiarity and trust that other reporters wouldn't have. Local businesses would be more inclined to run additional ads, I insisted, increasing the paper's revenue whenever they were the subject of an article. With that final comment, I could see I had him.

I shut up and waited for the verdict, jaw tight, nails digging into my palms to keep the ready tears from falling.

He smiled slightly and said, "You don't even know how to run the computers." Keep in mind, this was the 70s, and that wasn't the kind of ingrained skill it is today.

"If I learn by Sunday's deadline, can I be the Business Editor?"

The slight smile remained on his face for several seconds, seconds during which I could feel every beat of my wildly pulsing heart.

"Yes."

*He said yes!*

"But it's a trial basis and you'll have to do your other work, too."

I would have agreed to anything.

That evening I pestered the guys who worked in Sports—the only reporters who were working late—about how to run the computer. Terrified of making mistakes, but nonetheless determined, I pumped out the first double truck—with my title at the top of the page, just like I'd envisioned.

The Sunday issue, always our largest of the week, was printed in advance. The manager routinely looked through it to note the ads and check for any issues.

My desk sat kitty-corner to hers and I knew when she let out a loud huff that she'd turned to the new business section.

"Well, I never," she muttered.

Congratulations never came my way, nor was anything said about it for that matter, yet I celebrated.

Never again did I allow anyone to determine my path or drag me down to their expectations of me.

Here's what I want you to take away from my story.

- There's always a way to achieve what you want, even if it's not the path that others take.

- You have to believe in yourself even when no one else does.

- Look at the "why" behind what you want to do. If that "why" is large enough, it will be the touchstone that carries you through the rough times.

- Don't seek acclaim from others. Let your own satisfaction be enough.

- As George Edward Woodberry said, "Defeat is not the worst of failures. Not to have tried is the true failure."

As I look back at that time, I know how instrumental my efforts then were to my success today as an author of fifty-seven books and as a publisher of wonderful authors and their many successful books.

Each time you're faced with negative thoughts or a negative person, ask yourself, "If I don't try, will I regret it?" If the answer is yes, then *try*.

That's the primary thing I want you to take away from this book. Every entrepreneur here has experienced a situation like mine—one where only their belief in their own abilities brought about their success.

Ride on the shoulders of those who have paved the way. Each chapter will help you on your journey to be the magnificently successful businesswoman that you have within you.

# the
# MIND

*"Mindfulness can help people of any age. That's because we become what we think."*
GOLDIE HAWN

# Tools For Your Spirit

TONI CAYE SNYDER

When you feel the need, here are sixteen calming messages to return to.

## BELIEVE IN YOURSELF

Whether you feel that your business goals are a long way off or just a few moments away, it's essential that you feel confident that you can reach them. The key is to believe in yourself and your abilities. It's vital to embrace your intrinsic worth and uniqueness. You're constantly changing and developing, and there's no one else in the world quite like you. Your value is measured by how you perceive yourself.

There are many positive practices to help strengthen your belief in yourself. Spend some time highlighting your positive traits each day. Notice and shift the thought patterns that eat away at your self-esteem. Celebrate the small successes to remind yourself that you are more impressive than you give yourself credit for. Learn to listen to and accept compliments. Turn these recommendations into daily habits, and before you know it, you'll see your business goals become a reality.

## START YOUR DAY WITH POSITIVE SELF-TALK

A healthy way to improve your overall mindset is to start your day by saying positive things to yourself. What you express to yourself through words, thoughts, and images are interpreted on a deeper level than you may realize. Positive self-talk can shift your perspective by changing your limiting beliefs subconsciously. If you focus on a specific empowering belief long enough, eventually, the message will get through.

Spend some time being an active observer of your overall speech and thoughts. When you discover negativity in the way you're talking to yourself, focus on replacing negativity with positive things you want to hear. You can also consider repeating affirmations to help you turn your unwanted self-talk into something more hopeful and encouraging. Starting your day with an optimistic attitude enables you to accomplish your business dreams and goals with greater flow and ease.

## SUCCESS DOESN'T HAPPEN OVERNIGHT FOR ANYONE

Success doesn't happen overnight for anyone. It takes patience and persistence to build a business. There's no shortcut, quick fix, or magic button. You must have a strong desire to succeed and be willing to put in exceptional effort and dedication. Success requires courage, resilience, and a mindset that can endure trial and error. Determination to achieve your goals can carry you to new heights.

Progress comes in spurts, and it's easy to become frustrated. Spend your time and energy on what matters and give your efforts your full attention. Stay motivated by celebrating each time you check something off your to-do list, complete a project, raise your revenue, etc. Get support from like-minded people. Be consistent, and trust that positive results will come in time. Making progress means you're on the right track. Before long, you'll experience the success you've been dreaming about in your business.

## WHEN YOU'RE TEMPTED TO QUIT

The most successful people have a remarkable capacity to keep going when everyone else quits. Your success is tied to your ability to keep working after you have the urge to stop. Think about the reasons you feel like quitting, like lack of energy, not being able to focus, or not knowing your "why." If you're going to be one of the few who can persevere, you need to put one foot in front of the other.

You can stay motivated by revisiting your original purpose. Create small successes with easy goals that move you forward. Make a schedule that will ensure you remain engaged. Imagine how great you'll feel when you've reached a goal and ask yourself how you'll feel if you allow yourself to quit. Perseverance is the best indicator of your ability to be successful. You'll eventually succeed if you continue moving forward.

## REPLACING YOUR NEGATIVE VOICE

One of the most essential mindset shifts you can make for your business is to quiet your negative voice. Pessimistic, destructive self-talk disrupts your productivity and goals. You have numerous harmful conversations happening inside your head throughout the day, and this negativity can leave you feeling frustrated, angry, or defeated. The good news is that you can switch gears and redirect your unsupportive thoughts to more optimistic ones.

It's normal to have a cynical voice, so take a deep breath, acknowledge the thoughts, and try not to ignore them. Replace your negative thinking with more empowering statements. Start by changing "can't" to "can" and "I'm not" to "I am." For example, if you're saying, "I don't deserve success," change it to "I am inherently worthy of success." Repeat these positive words over and over again. The more you practice this, the better you'll get at silencing your negative voice.

## EMOTIONAL SUPPORT TEAM

It's natural to try to solve your problems on your own. Sometimes pride keeps you from asking for help, or it could be embarrassment or fear. However, you'll soon realize that you can solve your problems faster and more efficiently by joining or creating an emotional support team. The venting factor alone can make support teams worth it. Even if a solution may not exist, knowing others are in a similar situation can help you feel at ease.

A support team can help restore your confidence so you can reach your goals and give you the much-needed emotional release to open you up to a breakthrough. When you listen and relate to the support team members, you'll share real experiences from many different perspectives and become a better communicator. Find a group you can identify with and start looking forward to greater success today.

## THE IMPORTANCE OF REWARDING YOURSELF

Regardless of what you may have heard, embracing a healthy reward mindset will motivate you to work toward your goals. Rewarding yourself increases dopamine levels in your brain, which helps with executive function, mood regulation, and overall happiness. Dopamine is one of the reasons why you feel warm and fuzzy when you receive positive attention. And the more enhanced your emotional wellbeing, the more productive you'll be.

After completing a task or putting in a sufficient amount of work, find meaningful ways to reward yourself for your successes. Read the next chapter in a novel. Watch an episode of your favorite show. Get a spa treatment. Take a nap. Eat something yummy. Take a walk in nature. Enjoy a hobby. Chat with a friend. Rewarding yourself is a personal growth habit that will help boost your confidence, stay focused, reduce distractions, and give you the momentum to shoot for the stars.

## FINDING INSPIRATION

Research shows that when you experience higher amounts of inspiration, you'll have more precise goals and make more progress in realizing them. Inspiration transforms your task list from things you have to do into things you want to do. If you don't feel particularly inspired right now, changing your mindset, perspective, and scenery will welcome more inspiration into your life.

Sometimes you need to get creative when hunting for inspiration. Try practicing a positive attitude and focusing on the things you can control. Keep a gratitude journal to remind you of your blessings. Go somewhere you haven't been before to get a different perspective. Look at something you see every day differently or from a different angle. Close your eyes and seek inspiration in the sounds and smells around you. Feeling inspired will help you accomplish extraordinary things in a fun way so you can enjoy greater purpose, opportunity, and success.

## IT'S OKAY TO START OVER

Sometimes it's okay to start over. Hitting the reset button is a great option when you feel stuck, have a change of heart, realize the "fix" isn't a simple one, or just want to wipe the slate clean. If you decide the best course of action is to begin again, it's essential to set yourself up for success. Every day you try is another chance to achieve your goals.

Consider the reasons you want to start over and go forth with an optimistic mindset. Develop a new plan or a fresh approach. Set small, attainable objectives as well as a bigger goal that's appealing and inspiring. Build your confidence by performing tasks you know you're good at. Rekindle your motivation with a vision board, a gratitude visualization, or a pep talk from a friend. Reward your efforts often and remember that it's never too late to start . . . again.

## MISTAKES ARE A PART OF GROWTH

Mistakes are a part of growth. We all have to deal with various failures, defeats, and missteps. The key is to make the most of them by understanding and applying the lessons they teach. Each mistake carries the possibility of creating a lasting enhancement in your life. Embrace these opportunities for personal development.

The first step to success is to be honest with yourself and those involved about your mistake and hold yourself accountable. Without judgment or excessive rumination, think about the events and circumstances that led to the error, how you feel, and how it impacted others. Consider what you could have done differently to prevent your misstep and develop a solution if a similar situation occurs again. Reflect on what the mistake has taught you and how it has changed you for the better. Learning from and not repeating your mistakes will help you experience extraordinary personal growth.

## GETTING COMFORTABLE SAYING NO

If you feel you spend too much time on activities and responsibilities you don't enjoy, then saying "no" more often will bring some relief. There's a difference between someone who is open and accommodating and someone who says "yes" to everything. Always saying "yes" creates stress and eliminates your free time, interfering with your ability to create a thriving business. Start valuing yourself and your work by getting comfortable saying "no."

Saying "no" gives you more control over your life. When you say "yes" too much, you allow others to dictate your schedule. Declining a few requests will free up your time, and you'll have a better chance of achieving your goals. Saying "no" allows you to set boundaries so you can unwind and recharge. You'll have more to give if you take care of yourself, and you'll have more energy and attention to devote to your success.

## MARKING MILESTONES
Milestones motivate you to take on your next challenge by letting you see how far you've come and how much you've achieved. These landmarks show you an overview of your professional journey and keep track of your triumphs and victories, no matter how big or small. Milestones can be meaningful occasions that brighten your day or defining moments that signal you've arrived at the next stage in your business.

Take a moment to assess your memorable milestones. Observe all the "firsts", such as getting your first paying client or customer, selling your first product or program, or earning your first $1,000. Honor difficult tasks you've completed and goals you've attained. Note when you've stayed true to your word or positively impacted others. Mark when you've exceeded your expectations, surpassed your last performance, or accepted an award. Celebrating your victories will inspire you to create even bigger plans for your future.

## CLEARING BRAIN CLUTTER
Our lives are consumed with clutter, whether it's a chaotic kitchen drawer, a desk covered with papers, or an overwhelmed mind trying to deal with too much. A cluttered mind causes fatigue and results in inferior performance and poor decisions.

The good news is that you can declutter your mind, just as you can declutter your desk. The clutter in your head is under your control.

To help declutter your mind, start with your diet. Eat anti-inflammatory foods and keep your blood sugar stable. Get some exercise. Simplify your life and stop activities that don't add quality to your life or enjoyment. Create healthy daily and weekly routines to streamline your thought process. Prioritize and use your time advantageously to get the most important tasks accomplished. Give your mind regular breaks with quiet contemplation and meditation. With practice, you'll enjoy the benefits of more peace and clarity.

## LEARNING TO ASK FOR HELP

Many of us are hesitant to ask for help. Perhaps we feel embarrassed or ashamed to ask. Maybe we think it makes us look incapable or weak. But nothing could be farther from the truth. When you ask for help, you're being proactive and achieving a task or goal at a higher level than you could on your own. And most people will appreciate the chance to assist in a meaningful way.

Successful people understand that asking for help is efficient and saves time. You're not only faster with good support, but you can also perform better because there's someone out there who has more skill or talent. Getting help multiplies your efforts and results. It's an assertive behavior of people who take responsibility for their lives. So be bold, swallow your pride, and get comfortable asking for help with reaching your goals. You have so much to gain and so little to lose.

## MINDFULNESS PRACTICES

Mindfulness is the act of holding your attention solely on what you're doing right now and not thinking of other things.

Our lives are chaotic and busy, and we are so focused on the past and the future that we often forget to slow down and appreciate the small aspects of life. It only takes a few minutes of mindfulness to feel calmer and more grateful.

A quick mindfulness activity is to focus on one task and allow yourself to clear your mind, thinking of only how your body and senses are responding to the task. For example, drink a cup of tea, and consider how the tea tastes and how the warm cup feels in your hands. Go for a walk and appreciate the air's temperature and how the ground feels beneath your feet. Sit comfortably and notice what you see, feel, hear, smell, and taste. Take a mindfulness moment now and enjoy more peace and productivity.

## CREATING A PERSONAL AFFIRMATION
Some days it's challenging to think in an optimistic and success-affirming way. During these times, you can create your own personal affirmation statement to help shift your negative thinking and propel you toward your goals. Successful people use words like these to reprogram their thought processes and activate their minds to accomplish what they want to achieve.

Write your personal affirmation statement in the present tense with concise, positive words. For example, if you find that you're telling yourself what you "can't" do, you can replace those negative thoughts with affirmations such as "I have a great attitude for success", "I am worthy of great success", "I take pride in my small achievements", or "I can do this because I am energized and inspired." Feel into the energy of your affirmation, repeat it aloud several times, and reaffirm it to your subconscious to help you reach a higher level of success.

Toni Cay Snyder, PhD, is an accomplished Transformation Life Coach, Master Mindset Coach, and Meditation Mentor with over two decades of experience. She is passionate about empowering midlife women to overcome limiting beliefs, conquer obstacles, and create meaningful transformations in their personal and professional lives. Among her clients are international celebrities who have experienced significant positive changes under her guidance. Toni's holistic approach to coaching is a unique blend of mindset coaching, meditation practices, and wellness techniques that help her clients cultivate inner peace, clarity, and resilience. Her warmth, compassion, and innate understanding of human nature make her a trusted guide and confidante for anyone seeking to improve their life. When not coaching, Toni spends her free time enjoying the company of her kids and cats, exploring Colorado Springs, and indulging in her guilty pleasure of binge-watching K-dramas. https://tonicay.com/

*"Leadership is about making others better as a result of your presence and making sure that impact lasts in your absence."*
— SHERYL SANDBERG

# Harnessing the Power of Female Leadership in Entrepreneurship

## MARIE-JO CAESAR

As a financial wellness strategist and advocate for women in business, I firmly believe the future is female. Through my years of experience, I have seen firsthand the incredible potential that women bring to the business world. It's time to share that wisdom and knowledge with the young women who will shape our future.

I'll reveal the secrets to harnessing your unique strengths and perspectives to build thriving businesses. You'll learn from the successes of past and present female role models and discover achievable steps for success in business with a woman's touch. Together, we can inspire and nurture the next generation of female leaders and create a brighter, more equal future for all.

Let's make the future female!

## 1. LEARNING FROM OUR PAST AND PRESENT FEMALE LEADERS

History is filled with incredible women who have defied the odds to become leaders in their respective fields.

From Rosa Parks to Maya Angelou to Ruth Bader Ginsburg, every female trailblazer has a story filled with invaluable lessons on resilience, adaptability, and perseverance.

Just think for a minute if you were guided on your entrepreneurial journey by some of the most remarkable women in history. The challenges they faced, the triumphs they achieved, and the lessons they learned can all be translated into invaluable insights for anyone looking to make their mark in the world of business. These role models refused to be constrained by convention; they broke through endless obstacles and have left everlasting impressions on society. With their wisdom and inspiration, you, too, can carve out a path to success that is uniquely yours.

## 2. CULTIVATING LEADERSHIP QUALITIES AND RESILIENCE IN YOUNG WOMEN

To empower young women to become the leaders of tomorrow, we must first identify the key leadership qualities essential for success. These include adaptability, confidence, decisiveness, empathy, integrity, resilience, and vision.

Adaptability: In a constantly changing world, the ability to embrace change, learn from new experiences, and adjust strategies is essential for maintaining a competitive edge. Adaptive leaders are open-minded, resilient, and responsive to the evolving needs of their teams and organizations. They effectively navigate challenges, inspire innovation, and ensure long-term success in an ever-shifting landscape.

Confidence: Confident leaders inspire trust and motivate team members to achieve their goals. This quality helps leaders navigate challenges, instill optimism, and drive an organization toward progress and growth.

Decisiveness: In a world where the tide of change never stops, speedy and informed decision-making becomes a critical need.

A true leader who values both sides of every argument chooses confidently, takes ownership of the results, and inspires trust in their team. By nailing the perfect balance between being strong without being impetuous, leaders instill their teams with absolute confidence. When turbulence rocks the boat, decisive leadership acts like a rock, providing the stability and momentum that lead to prosperity.

Empathy: It is not just a feel-good quality, as it is quintessential for leaders to understand the needs and feelings of their team members, customers, and stakeholders. That is the kind of leader we need in today's world.

Integrity encompasses honesty, trustworthiness, and strong moral principles, forming the foundation for authentic and ethical decision-making. Ultimately, integrity shapes the character of a leader and plays a pivotal role in driving an organization's success and reputation.

Resilience distinguishes great leaders from ordinary ones. Resilient leaders are capable of withstanding hardship and rebound from unforeseen obstacles, rendering them tenacious and adaptable. They confront challenges upfront, use them as opportunities for advancement, and exhibit unparalleled determination, inspiring their teams to keep going, and they instill a culture of fearlessness and perseverance.

Vision: A successful leader has the ability to foresee future possibilities and craft a compelling, purposeful course for an organization that inspires and motivates others to follow and work towards a common goal.

To nurture these qualities, I will urge you future female leaders to seek out mentors, engage in personal development programs, and continuously invest in your growth. You must embrace lifelong learning and strive to be the best version of yourselves.

## 3. EMBRACING INNOVATION AND CONTINUOUS IMPROVEMENT

In the ever-evolving world of business, stay informed about technologies, market changes, and emerging trends such as artificial intelligence (AI). Be open to new ideas and approaches, and always strive to refine and enhance your business model.

As a female leader, your ability to adapt and innovate will not only drive your business forward, but also inspire others to follow in your footsteps.

## 4. ADOPTING FINANCIAL LITERACY AND EMPOWERMENT

Financial literacy and empowerment hold paramount significance for you as a successful leader in today's fast-paced, ever-evolving world. Once you master the complexities of financial management, including budgeting, investing, and risk mitigation, you will be able to adeptly navigate the intricate landscape of business growth and sustainability. Because when you have a strong grasp on the nuances of financial decision-making, you can allocate resources efficiently, ensuring optimal returns on investments. Concurrently, you can adeptly identify and seize lucrative opportunities, propelling your organization to new heights. Financial empowerment, intrinsically tied to financial literacy, enables you to confidently make informed choices that drive long-term prosperity. Undeniably, financial literacy and empowerment serve as vital cornerstones in the foundation of your exceptional leadership.

## 5. PROMOTING WORK-LIFE HARMONY

Achieving work-life harmony is essential for you as a successful leader as it allows you to maintain a delicate equilibrium between your professional aspirations and personal well-being. It is essential to consciously prioritize and nurture both aspects of your life so you can effectively prevent burnout and foster a healthier and more resilient mindset. Ultimately, as you embrace work-life harmony, you cultivate an environment where creativity, innovation, and productivity can thrive, and you pave the way for sustainable success and satisfaction in both your professional and personal spheres.

## 6. INVESTING IN YOURSELF AND YOUR COMMUNITY

To truly make a lasting impact and inspire the next generation of women leaders, you must invest in yourself and your community. This means dedicating time, resources, and energy to personal growth, education, and mentorship programs that empower young women to pursue their dreams and achieve their full potential. Ultimately, this investment in self-improvement and community empowerment will solidify your reputation as a compassionate and visionary leader.

## 7. BUILDING SUPPORTIVE NETWORKS AND ENCOURAGING ALLIANCES

Networking and mentorship are critical components to the success of any entrepreneur, particularly women. Make sure to establish strong professional relationships as they will not only provide valuable guidance but also open doors to new opportunities. Actively participate in networking events, join professional associations, and connect with like-minded individuals on social media platforms.

Additionally, male allies play a vital role in promoting gender equality and supporting women entrepreneurs. So, encourage men in your network to champion women's rights and advocate for their advancement, and by fostering an environment of inclusivity and collaboration, you can create a more equitable business landscape.

## 8. LEVERAGING THE POWER OF DIVERSE REPRESENTATION

Embracing the power of diverse representation is a game-changer for you as a successful leader, as championing inclusivity and welcoming varied perspectives allows you to foster an environment where innovation thrives and creativity flourishes. And recognizing and appreciating the unique strengths that everyone brings to the table strengthens your credibility as a forward-thinking and transformative leader. Harnessing diversity, you'll drive your organization to unparalleled heights of success.

## 9. OVERCOMING CHALLENGES AND BARRIERS FACED BY WOMEN ENTREPRENEURS

Women entrepreneurs often face unique challenges, such as access to funding, gender bias, and balancing work-life responsibilities. To overcome these barriers and arm yourself with knowledge and resources and seek guidance from mentors who have navigated similar obstacles.

Moreover, as a leader you have a unique opportunity to champion gender equality in the workplace and beyond. So, support the implementation of inclusive policies and practices, and the promotion of diversity in your organization. Also, address any instances of bias or discrimination, and advocate for equal pay, equal opportunities, and equal representation for women in your industry. Most importantly, use your voice to effect change.

## 10. CELEBRATING AND SHARING SUCCESS STORIES

Acknowledging our achievements and sharing our stories is essential for inspiring future generations and elevating women in business. As you break through barriers and forge new paths, you pave the way for the next generation of women leaders. By openly celebrating your successes, you validate your hard work and perseverance and provide valuable inspiration and motivation for others to follow in your footsteps.

As I conclude, I will say that it is up to us, as current leaders, mentors, and role models, to ignite the spark of ambition within the hearts and minds of young women, allowing them to visualize themselves as the trailblazers of tomorrow.

The future of female leadership isn't just about giving women more power; it's also about changing our society, challenging norms, and accepting diversity in all its forms. So, you can't afford to be complacent. The time is now.

I am the proud owner and founder of Merging Life and Money, a financial wellness company. As a seasoned businesswoman and a devoted family member, I am all about helping busy professionals aged 35 to 60+ break free from destructive financial and emotional habits. I will equip you with the right skills and knowledge to take charge of your finances and live your best life with the money you have. Trust me, my unique and proven Merging Life and Money™ method delivers results—guaranteed!

I am incredibly passionate about empowering others by sharing my expertise. My mission? To continue providing top-notch financial wellness solutions for individuals and companies alike. So, if you are ready to transform your financial future, let's start this journey together! You will not be disappointed.

**The Leadership Compass: Navigating Your Way to Success with Timeless Wisdom** is a curated collection of wisdom from successful female leaders, designed to ignite your entrepreneurial spirit and strengthen your leadership qualities, as you navigate the challenges of personal and professional growth.

https://mariejocaesar.com/the-leadership-compass

*"The future belongs to those who believe in the beauty of their dreams."*
– ELEANOR ROOSEVELT

# The Perspective of Possibility

CINNAMON ALVAREZ

L ike life, business can be both fun and challenging. Remarkably, it can be both simultaneously! Entrepreneurs often overlook or underestimate the perspective of possibility—a way of thinking that opens our minds to potential by looking at the world with a sense of optimism and opportunity, instead of restrictions. This perspective of possibility bolsters our self-confidence, encouraging us to pursue our business goals with determination.

The power of positive thinking has been widely studied and documented, and the evidence is clear: entrepreneurs with a mindset of possibility are more likely to achieve greater success than those with a limited view of the world. A study conducted by the University of Pennsylvania and the Wharton School showed that entrepreneurs with a "growth mindset" are more likely to display entrepreneurial qualities such as creativity, innovation, and risk-taking, and are thus more successful in their endeavors than those with a "fixed mindset" (the belief that abilities are predetermined). Other research has found that entrepreneurs with higher levels of positive thinking tend to have higher levels of self-efficacy and optimism, which are essential for success in business. Additionally, studies have demonstrated that those with higher levels of positive thinking tend to be more creative and innovative, which can be invaluable for finding creative solutions to challenging problems. It's no wonder those with higher levels of positive thinking often go on to achieve great things in their endeavors! With the right mindset and the right attitude, anything is possible.

You may already be aware of the fact that our mindset has a huge impact on everything we do, feel, and experience. This is not a new concept. However, understanding the value of a positive mindset and actively applying it to generate a perspective of possibility is a very different challenge. This is a skill that can be learned and developed. So, how can you increase your confidence, drive, and ability to look beyond the current conditions, think innovatively, and come up with creative solutions? I am going to provide tips on how to maximize the effectiveness of harnessing the perspective of possibility based on my experience as a successful long-term business owner. To begin with, here are some simple steps you can incorporate into your daily routine to help you make possibility-thinking a habit.

1. **Make an effort to open your mind to new ideas, solutions, and perspectives.** Read books, attend seminars, and network with people who can offer different points of view. (You're reading this book, so you're already on the right track.)

2. **Keep a journal.** Take time to daydream and mentally paint the future you'd like to create. Write out goals and possible ways to accomplish them. Take time to reflect on lessons learned and opportunities to grow and become better. Write down things you are grateful

for. If you use your journal as a to-do list, consider renaming your to-dos your "list of good intentions," which will reduce any guilt you may feel about not accomplishing every item.

3. **Practice mindfulness and exercise.** Use meditation and mindful breathing to bring a sense of calm and clarity and to become aware of your thoughts. Add exercise to boost your can-do attitude; there's often a moment in the middle of a workout when you feel the switch from feeling like it's impossible to feeling like you can do anything. (It's the perfect time for generating business ideas.)

4. **Implement a structure to actively create your day.** I host a group "generating call" every weekday morning in which each participant creates a mindset for the day and three actionable goals. Each following day, we report on our success or failure in accomplishing these goals and generate new ones. I find our calls to be especially helpful with creating new opportunities and outcomes I may not have considered.

Through regular practice, cultivating the perspective of possibility becomes more instinctive. Even with over two decades of experience and four successful businesses under my belt, I still experience anxiety, feel overwhelmed, and get discouraged at times. Nevertheless, it becomes easier to switch from a "can't do" attitude to a "can do" one. My ability to bring forth what I like to call a "Game-On Mindset" and actively look at life and business through the perspective of possibility has been a tremendous factor in my success. For instance, I've had a competitor offer my customers money and free products to switch suppliers. I couldn't compete with their deep pockets, but strategizing that led to the development of new, unique products that were difficult to knock off—and diversifying our customer base was rewarding. It is my hope that with a bit of effort, you too can tap into the power of the perspective of possibility and create more success in your life and business.

The human mind is truly fascinating, with its seemingly limitless complexity and capacity to process, reason, store, and recall vast amounts of information. Our thoughts have the power to direct the course of our lives, for better or for worse. We can choose to cultivate a mindset of possibility, unlocking our potential and allowing us to reach our goals in business and life, or we can get caught up in self-preservation and doubt our own capabilities, making assumptions about others in the process. For example, if you lose a big customer, you could ruminate over things you should have done differently, letting it keep you up at night. Alternatively, you could notice your inner critic and defense mechanisms kicking in, find that fascinating and acknowledge your fear, then rapidly get back on your feet by reaching out to even better business prospects. Inquisitiveness is a powerful tool that should not be underestimated; it allows us to become aware of our thoughts and evaluate their accuracy, instead of being emotionally drawn into them. Inquisitiveness helps us confront our restrictive beliefs, open our minds to new possibilities and, ultimately, cultivate possibility.

Difficult circumstances can be challenging, but they can also offer a valuable gift. In my experience, I've found that people are often eager to escape the discomfort of negative emotions, thus missing out on the opportunity to recognize how deeply they care about something. For example, my brother was diagnosed with paranoid schizophrenia when we were teens. To say the least, it was heartbreaking to watch him turn to street drugs instead of prescribed medication and be institutionalized and incarcerated time and time again. I couldn't fix the situation and I could only begin to imagine what his experience was like. I loved my brother; I knew that. So, each and every opportunity from then on, I was grateful for any chance to express my love for him, and that's what I did until he died. I still feel sad from time to time, but the love in my heart always prevails. And not just for my brother, but for humanity. I'm now comfortable wearing my heart on my sleeve and I express my gratitude often. Self-compassion and honoring emotions such as sadness, anger, and frustration can help us better understand our passions and desires. It can increase our capacity to handle stress and face life's challenges with greater resilience. Plus, it can help us tap into our passion, know what's important to us, and make a difference in the world. So, don't be afraid to show yourself a little compassion and kindness—it can be the driving force behind your success!

Being mindful of our self-talk is key to cultivating a perspective of possibility. Our words have power and are a great indicator of either limited thinking or possibility thinking. Notice what you're saying to yourself; if you're using words like "can't", "have to", or "need to", these are all limiting beliefs. On the other hand, words like "can", "could", or "will" evoke a sense of possibility and open us to new opportunities. Switching from a pessimistic mindset of "can't do" to an optimistic outlook of "can do" can be difficult. To help with this, I created a "Mental Renovation" process, which is a practice of consciously choosing our words and thoughts to transform negative rumination and turn our self-talk around. You may have heard Brene Brown use the term "The story I'm telling myself." I like to use "It seems like…" to dump my frustrations onto paper and introduce possibilities for change. I then omit disempowering language, identify my intentions, and make a new declaration. This renovation process is incredibly useful in cultivating a mindset of possibility, discovering more empowering options, and getting into action.

Having a robust perspective of possibility is essential for accomplishing big business goals. By looking at examples of the seemingly impossible being achieved, we can help replace limited thinking with a new, more expansive perspective. One such example is the breaking of the four-minute mile. Before Roger Bannister, running a four-minute mile was thought to be impossible due to the physical strain it would require. Yet, just forty-six days after he broke the record, John Landy managed to do it in three minutes and 57.9 seconds. Since then, over 1,400 other athletes have managed to run a sub-four-minute mile, proving the power of hard work, dedication, and self-belief. This serves as an inspirational reminder of our capacity to accomplish big goals by expanding our perspective of what's possible. It is equally, if not more important, to look for those with whom we can relate. Finding someone successful with a similar background who makes us think "I can do that" can be a powerful way to ignite our own ambition.

Many people are willing to give advice—some unsolicited and some less helpful than others! But when it comes to launching or growing a business, it pays to seek those who have achieved remarkable success repeatedly. Not only can they provide valuable insight into industry trends, best practices, and potential pitfalls, but they also offer an external point of view. A mentor who's already navigated a new market can be an invaluable asset in reducing the time it takes to reach success. Never underestimate the power of expert guidance. Trust a mentor's advice but verify the facts as well. (I learned this the hard way.) After all, it's your business, so you want to make decisions that are in your best interest.

Accomplishing big goals can seem daunting, but it can be done one step at a time. Prioritizing progress over perfection can help you avoid getting stuck in a cycle of over-correcting. Even the smallest adjustments and micro-moves can make a tremendous impact, as Stephen Covey explains in his book *The Seven Habits of Highly Effective People*, using the example of how hitting a golf ball in a slightly different spot can make it go in a completely different direction. Visualize your desired outcome, then ask yourself what actionable step can be taken to get one step closer to your goal. Taking small, consistent steps, even if they seem insignificant, can help build your confidence to tackle the bigger tasks. Additionally, be aware of any tasks that you may be avoiding, as these may be the most valuable. Taking action is key. Like my favorite mantra espouses, "slow and steady wins the race." By taking deliberate action, one small step at a time, you will eventually reach your big goals.

Last but not least, my own "unsolicited advice" on leveraging the perspective of possibility to build a successful business is this: As you strive to build a successful business, remember that your work is not only a contribution to your own success, but to society at large. Your products and services can benefit people in many ways, from providing necessary goods and services, to improving people's quality of life, to creating jobs and economic opportunities. Your business can also generate tax revenue that supports essential public services, such as schools and libraries, and contributes to a stronger, more connected community. You have what it takes, you are worthy, and the sky's the limit. Thank you for your vision and mission, and for the positive impact your business makes. Here's to your continued success!

Cinnamon is a passionate advocate of social entrepreneurship, dedicating her life to helping people make a positive impact through their work. She has built four successful businesses, including her thriving ceramic lighting manufacturing company A19, an art gallery, a fitness franchise, and World Changemaker, where she co-facilitates the R.O.I. (Raising One's Impact) Retreat. In addition, she authored the bestselling book *Generating Your Own Happiness*, and serves on her local Workforce Development Board. Cinnamon's commitment to service has been recognized in the following honors: The NEWH Award of Excellence and Network of Outstanding Women Motivator Award. However, she considers the greatest award to be the one which comes from helping others and seeing them make a difference in the world.

Mental Renovation Worksheet. A "mental renovation" is a fundamental practice to change your perception of your current circumstances and generate specific outcomes. A renovation invites your mind to have a different experience of life and create different, more empowering options. This is a foundational tool for generating your own happiness and cultivating the perspective of possibility for more empowering options.

Get your free "Mental Renovation" Worksheet at

https://thepublishingcircle.com/happiness

*"With realization of one's own potential and self-confidence in one's ability, one can build a better world."*
— THE DALAI LAMA

# The Confidence Habit

## DIANN WINGERT

O ne of the subjects I have been most obsessed with throughout my career, first as a psychotherapist, and more recently as a business coach, is women and confidence.

Of the countless girls and women I've known, no matter how accomplished they were, the vast majority lacked genuine confidence. I began to study the subject and the more I learned, the more perplexed I became. At first I assumed it was an issue of competency and achievement, but I turned out to be wrong. In the U.S., more women earn college and advanced degrees than men. We have made some progress in closing the wage gap, but women still hold back from pursuing opportunities they're qualified for. Unless they believe they're 100% qualified, they opt out and go into a less competitive area or field. Obviously, all men are not confident, but according to considerable published research, they don't let their doubts stop them nearly as frequently as women do.

In 2012, Columbia University professor Ernesto Rueben coined the term "honest overconfidence" to describe how men rated their performance about thirty percent better than it actually is. Women tend to experience the opposite—imposter syndrome—underestimating their abilities and attributing their success to luck or circumstance. What women have not understood is that competency and hard work aren't enough. Confidence is also necessary because it makes you stand out and helps you rise. Women tend to accept the blame when things go wrong and often credit luck or other people when they succeed—the opposite of what most men do. In general, men take risks, make mistakes, learn from them, and course-correct, while women perpetually hold back, and don't take action until they feel they are ready. The trait of perfectionism results in wasted time and missed opportunities because while some women are trying to get it "just right", others are taking imperfect action and moving forward.

I am fascinated by this area of science, as well as the entire topic of gender identity and social conditioning, which is becoming an increasingly complex and controversial subject. My goal in writing this is not to spark a debate, but to normalize the frustrating phenomenon experienced by countless women, including myself. If you are a woman who has struggled with confidence, you are definitely not alone and it is also not your fault. The struggle begins in your brain. Compared to men's brains, women's brains have, in general, stronger memories of negative events, and the fight-or-flight response is more easily triggered in the amygdala. This also increases the likelihood of rumination—replaying the past over and over, a form of "perfectionism after the fact." Not only do we expect to say and do things perfectly, but we also torment ourselves when we don't.

Another part of the brain, the anterior cingulate cortex, helps us recognize mistakes and also helps us weigh options. Well, guess what? It's larger in women, leading us to be more prone to worry and anxiety. Our ancient ancestors needed to recognize risk and danger because of procreation and child-rearing. But now, in the modern world, women tend to worry and overthink, have difficulty making decisions, second guess decisions they've made, and miss opportunity after opportunity, because they don't want to get it wrong. So they hold back. Tendencies that are thought of as "feminine", such as being collaborative instead of competitive and having enhanced emotional intelligence, are literally wired into us. But unless women are willing to make mistakes and learn from them and deal with conflict better, we will not be able to catch up to men.

Hormones also play a role. Higher levels of testosterone equate to more risk-taking, and men have ten times more testosterone than women. Taking risks increases the chances of success, success produces more testosterone, and the cycle continues. Women don't need to start taking testosterone to learn how to take more risks, but just understanding that much of what we're up against is biological can help women take some of the pressure off of ourselves for not feeling or acting with as much confidence as we would like.

But what about the environment? Girls begin elementary school with an upper hand in respect to socialization and the more easily we can be socialized, the more we begin to crave approval, which we get by being good. The result is that many girls learn to avoid making mistakes and taking risks because being a good girl gets them positive attention and social approval, which may pay off in the classroom, but it does not prepare them for the real world. Many psychologists now believe risk-taking, failure, and perseverance are the essential building blocks to confidence. Boys get scolded more, get punished more, and get sent to the principal's office more, but the majority of them learn to take failure in stride.

Many parents believe playing sports is good for kids, but I was surprised to learn just how extensive the benefits really are with respect to confidence. Girls who played team sports are more likely to graduate from college, more likely to find a job, are more likely to be employed in male-dominated industries, and also tend to earn more as adults than girls who did not play team sports. Learning to enjoy both victory and defeat in sports turns out to be good training for surviving setbacks in business and in life. According to the Centers for Disease Control, girls are still six times more likely to drop out of team sports and the steepest decline in their participation is during adolescence. This is probably linked to the fact that girls suffer a larger decrease in self-esteem during their teen years than boys do.

What a vicious circle! Girls lose confidence, so they quit competing, thereby depriving themselves of one of the best ways to retain it. They finish school, proving they can study hard, get good grades, and are determined to please, but somewhere between the classroom and the boardroom, the rules changed and most females don't recognize it. The requirements for adult success are different, and as a result, women's confidence takes a beating. Confidence is not just feeling good about yourself. Confidence is the ability to read the room, calibrate our own behavior, and keep our eye on the prize.

In looking at the different definitions for confidence, I think the one that makes the most sense and the definition I think is the most functional is this: "confidence is the belief in one's ability to succeed." This belief stimulates action and taking action bolsters our belief in our ability to succeed. As a result, confidence accumulates. This is the essence of what I call the confidence habit.

I believe all behavior is habit forming. So, in order to become more confident, women need to stop thinking so much and act more quickly. We need to commit to doing work that is good enough instead of perfect. We must learn to act before we think we are ready and surround ourselves with other women who are doing the same. By practicing behaviors associated with confidence, we can make confidence a habit and not an elusive reward.

So, where do you start? Follow the confident women on social media, listen to their podcasts, read their blogs and their books, take their courses, and meet them in real life. Notice how they think, how they act, how they make decisions, and the way they carry themselves physically. Then borrow the behaviors and traits you admire and practice them until they start to feel like your own. Confidence is not a reward for being a good girl or doing a good job. We simply got that all wrong. Confidence is a decision. It is a habit. And with practice, any behavior can become natural and effortless.

After a while, your brain will create actual physical structures called neural pathways that will help maintain the confident habit with much less effort and intention. Once your brain has these neural pathways in place, you will notice you are acting confident, feeling confident, and doing the things a confident woman does much more frequently and naturally.

Hesitancy, perfectionism, overthinking, rumination, fear of failure, and imposter syndrome might come more easily to women, but we can outsmart these tendencies and choose to develop our confidence. Because women tend to be more collegial than competitive, look for opportunities to be around other women who also want to become more confident. Changing our mindset and behavior can take time, and being part of a supportive community—even if it is with just one other woman who shares your goals—will enhance your ability to stick with it and persevere. You have no way of knowing what opportunities await you when you are willing to adopt the confidence habit.

Diann Wingert became a business strategist and coach after a twenty-year career as a psychotherapist. She is obsessed with helping women overcome the obstacles that hold them back, including procrastination, perfectionism, and people pleasing. In her 1:1 and group coaching programs, Diann's mission is to help female solopreneurs with big ideas and busy brains get focused, fired up, and become flame retardant. She is the creator of The Boss Up Breakthrough System and host of The Driven Woman Entrepreneur Podcast. Diann loves helping women transfer their success in their corporate, nonprofit, or academic career to create a stand-out, sought-after, and profitable business based on their brilliance. Diann is a Peloton enthusiast, dog mama, profane Buddhist, word nerd, and according to one of her favorite clients, "The Speaker of Uncomfortable Truths." She has been told her coaching approach is the perfect combination of "a kick in the pants and a warm hug."

"Unlearn" playing small and settling. Here's a link to get your free copy of The Confidence Habit. It's never too late to learn to be more confident to uplevel your business and life!

https://www.diannwingertcoaching.com/the-confidence-habit

# Existential Risk for Fast Results & Radical Business Building

WENDY BARR

**M**ost small businesses require the leader of the company to wear many hats. You need to work "in" your business every day to fulfill client orders, keep the books, order supplies, advertise and market, pay the bills, and hire/train your employees. In addition, you need to work "on" your business with future planning around product development, program offerings, budgets for sustainability, new technology, learning curves, and creative business strategies for growth and expansion, among other tasks! Your bandwidth can become spread pretty thin, pretty fast.

The secret to success, however, is in your ability to focus your efforts on key projects, strategies, and systems that get you where you're going to produce fast results. In Barrcode Branding, that's why we created a multitude of detailed workbooks, based on our actual client needs, challenges, overall struggles, and big wins.

For example, we noticed we were investing a great deal of time educating our individual clients on Business and Brand Basics (working "in" our business) and recognized the value of stepping back to create an educational series (working "on" our business) that allowed everyone on-demand access to their burning business development questions that needed answers right away.

Structuring the time to focus on building this out took effort, but the results speak for themselves. Not only does it educate prospects and clients alike, it creates a duplicatable system, an opportunity for additional income, and it frees up our time to focus on other exciting projects.

It's sad how often really spectacular business ideas fail for lack of planning. We said it before and we'll say it again, "Make no mistake, if you're building a business, you're building a brand."

**How would you rate your current business model?**

- Do you have clear mission/vision statements?

- Have you developed your core brand values?

- Do you have solid financial planning for sustainable growth?

- Can you highlight your unique distinctions in the marketplace?

- Can you describe your dream client in detail?

- Have you developed irresistible offers that compel and sell?

- How cohesive are your branding and marketing assets and strategies?

- Is your visual identity system cohesive, contemporary, and relevant?

We hope you answered yes and great to all the above! But if you answered, "I don't have time for that right now. I have a business to run", how do you expect to compete in the long-term with those who take the time to build out a solid, sustainable, scalable business model from the start?

**Here are some tips & tricks to help your business stand out:**

**Build a brand.** You need much more than just a logo. People don't buy products and/or services, they buy brands. Over the last few years, the relationship between consumers and brands has changed and evolved dramatically. Where a logo used to be enough, now there is this desire for a human dynamic between the two that never really existed before. Why be average when you can be outstanding?

**Connect with humans.** With social media, AI, and digital engagement being so prominent, the consumer is looking for connection and transparency. They want to know what your brand stands for. Today's consumer wants more. They have big expectations from the brands they support. All this information needs to be well established for the business brand before any attempt at marketing can be successful.

**Know your unique distinctions.** Spend some time with a branding agency that can help you distinguish your brand, tell your story, and create a unique experience for your clients. Identifying your unique distinctions and brand personality in advance will fuel all future strategic planning and lay the groundwork for your business growth, hiring, methodology, and product launches.

**Maximize your reach.** Normalize your brand so it's inclusive of demographics that might not otherwise explore your brand. These are serious consumers that have the potential to spend a lot of money, so you need to be inclusive and approachable.

**A picture speaks 1000 words.** For a consistent look and feel that consumers take seriously, have a professional agency design your branded visuals. Keep in mind that your branding, in all its forms, will dictate the look and feel of your collateral material and marketing-related design assets.

**Simple is best.** Remember, it takes about seven seconds to make a great first impression, and you only get one chance, so make sure your brand messaging speaks directly to your ideal client. Use consistent colors, fonts, and imagery relevant to the personality of your brand and communicate quickly and effectively with your ideal consumer. It's really all about creating an interesting and compelling business brand that makes people want to learn more.

**Keep up your momentum.** This is where you build recognition and authority through your value, offer, delivery, client journey, voice, and visuals. Keep in mind that successful businesses do a rebrand or brand refresh every three to five years and twenty to thirty percent of their annual budget is earmarked for branding and marketing. This type of consistent budgeting results in brand awareness and a substantial annual ROI. Trust me, it's worth it.

The truth is, small business owners often skip this crucial step.

If you want to compete with industry leaders, you need to take stock of what is and isn't working in your business model. The fastest way to get those answers is to ask those questions!

We have clients who never, yes we said never, go to market with a new product/service until they have deeply researched the need for that product/service. Big businesses do this all the time, with entire budgets dedicated to paying people to research and analyze the industry so they can spend their business development dollars wisely.

Yes, most entrepreneurs often skip this crucial step, and it costs them dearly every time. We've heard all the excuses: "I'm too busy/I don't know WHAT to ask/I don't know WHO to ask." And we've heard statements like these: "I'm sure everyone needs my product." Or "I know what I do, isn't that enough?"

It can actually be rewarding and insightful to get to know what your prospects are really looking for in your products/ services. Learning that can save time in the long run if you make a few personal connections who provide that kind of input on the front end.

**OUTCOMES of doing your due diligence:**

1. Save $$ and Time. There's no wasted energy on products that aren't appealing or marketable.

2. You create products/services with higher ROI. Better products equal a higher price tag.

3. You can gain new clients simply by having this market research conversation with a prospect, or even a total stranger. That happens all the time.

4. Market research opens the door to referral partners and engages loyal clients in the process.

5. Taking time to conduct due diligence provides you with more exposure and stronger credibility. This gives you a great opportunity to share your expertise in a non-salesy way.

If you've been in business for any time at all, you know making money is a numbers game. You can call it enrollment, sales, and/or buying in, but in the end, if you are exchanging your services for money, it is a sale.

Branding and marketing encompass all that is necessary to promote your business products and services, but it only works if you work it. It's critical to know the value of what you offer, both as it relates to the client and as it provides a sustainable business income.

Every business, new and growing, must first know exactly what's needed financially to survive and to thrive. Then, you must create compelling offers around your products that appeal to your target market and make it easy for them to say yes. So, know your numbers, even if you don't like math!

If nothing else, hear this: you need to get comfortable promoting your business every day, all the time! The internet makes it affordable to communicate broadly about your business through social channels and paid advertising, but it can never take the place of personal connections—never.

Research shows that you have only seven seconds to capture someone's attention. Forget your "elevator pitch", forget your spectacular products and services, forget even introducing yourself . . . people decide quickly whether or not learning more about you fits into their tight schedule.

Today's consumer is savvy. They want to support businesses that consider humans and the greater world when making business decisions. The internet allows the consumer to pop the hood and look inside.

They want to "meet the boss" whenever possible. Map out a plan to make yourself available to your ideal prospect. Offer authentic communication, both online and in person. Heck, go ahead and do something crazy, like picking up the phone and calling them personally.

At this point, you may be asking yourself, "Is my business brand working for me or against me?" Or even "My business is doing okay, but could my branding be the reason I haven't made it to the next level?" Whether you are growing a new business or scaling an established one, these are valid questions.

Wendy Barr is the CEO and Creative Director at Barrcode Branding, a leading branding agency with an innovative approach to human branding.

Pioneering a fresh new perspective on branding, Wendy believes people want to do business with other people, and they want the brands they choose to be in alignment with their personal value system.

Wendy has a Master's degree in branding and design. She has worked with some of the world's leading brands, such as MTV networks, Nickelodeon, RCA Records, Allure Magazine, Rockefeller Center, P Diddy, and more. She is an accomplished stage speaker and enjoys helping brilliant business owners build a human brand that connects emotionally with their target audience so they can attract their ideal client like a magnet, make more money, and impact the world!

When she's not at the office, she's traveling, going to rock concerts, walking her dog, taking stand-up comedy classes, having fun, and getting her laugh on!

Your value proposition statement or elevator pitch is often the first thing a prospective client encounters when exploring your brand. It explains your unique distinctions, the value you offer, and quickly and succinctly shares the solutions you provide. Boom, they choose YOU!

We'd like to help you get some "insider info" on how to create a powerful Value Proposition Statement (elevator pitch)! Click here to download your free VPS Formula Guide!

https://www.barrcodebranding.com/vpsformula

*"It's a mistake to believe the happiest people have had easy lives. The truth is that they've survived the worst of times and choose to be happy."*
COLONEL DEB LEWIS

# Life is Tough for Women Entrepreneurs: Be TougHer

## COLONEL DEB LEWIS

A panicked "no!" A savage scream. An indignant roar. All clear signs a woman entrepreneur has just been pushed beyond her limits.

Uh oh! Her office door swings open. She steps out of her office.

What will she do next?

Like most people, she hasn't been taught how to handle stressful moments; we might as well roll the dice.

You can imagine what lessons I learned after thirty-four years in a man's world. I rose to key leadership positions as a colonel and Army Engineer, enhanced by more than a decade working with academia, non-profits, and businesses.

What's the biggest difference I found in predicting long-term success or failure? How well each person handled stress. In other words, the greatest leaders formed the strongest relationships through mutual trust. The ability to keep their cool, even under extreme stress, inspires everyone to share their best.

**How well you handle stressful moments frees you to consistently give your best and bring out the best in everyone around you.**

It's easy to spot the unprepared . . . and it's not pretty!

This book was created to help you be a successful entrepreneur. Take the time and get ready for what you'll face in the days and months ahead. A little preparation goes a long way.

You may wish for a smooth and easy journey. Know that when you can successfully handle the hard times and everything in between, these important lessons will produce your greatest rewards.

**Hard times offer rich opportunities.**

Ready for more?

Just as I chose to serve in the military, your entrepreneurship path is not for the faint of heart. In today's stress-filled world, women are already at greater risk of feeling overwhelmed, alone, and stuck by life's adversities.

Expect to be tested in all sorts of ways—mentally, physically, and emotionally. My military career prepared me to lead in combat, but not before I was knocked down, attacked, and put down at least 10,000 times. Wow! People who don't handle stress well can be mean!

I learned a lot as my sisters-in-arms and I blazed a trail for over 5,000 women who have since followed. My greatest joy and toughest test would come years later: motherhood—a story for another day.

**Prepare daily for the bigger obstacles ahead of you.**

I admit, the obstacle course at West Point took me four long years to figure out. Progress was not a straight line, and my height and strength put me at a disadvantage. Still, it meant so much when I finally achieved an A+.

I learned early on to use every experience to better prepare for what's ahead. I've battle-tested and continuously refined my approach to stress every day. I really love finding faster ways to achieve amazing outcomes others consider impossible and not worth pursuing.

When I chose to attend the Military Academy at West Point in the first class with women, I was forced to adapt quickly under extreme stress. What helped? Before arriving, I established clear goals and told myself not to make long-term decisions when in an emotional state, especially while upset or angry.

**Identify what's most important before your next crisis. It carries you past intense hardships.**

Talk about marching into history and getting whacked! My most valuable insights came at a huge cost that I prefer no one else repeat.

You've likely dealt with a lot in your own life or you wouldn't be reading this now. My commitment is to make it easier for you to handle life's unexpected setbacks. When the smiles return to people I've coached, it sure makes all the hard work and difficult days worthwhile.

The keys to my success may sound obvious and simple; that's intentional. Sadly, they are not common practice nor widely understood . . . yet! You can help share this knowledge to improve lives and accomplish more in spite of the needy, stress-filled world that tests us. Get excited about what's next.

**Once understood, simple small shifts can make a huge difference.**

Let's revisit our entrepreneur as she walks out of her office to consider what might be going on.

Under added stress and without strategies or stress tools that work quickly, logic and wisdom soon fly out the window. Our well-being suffers when we become stressed out and negative emotions dominate. Where negativity flourishes, it creates unhealthy workplaces and homes. Every day, businesses lose a fortune in profits due to a growing number of combative, disengaged, actively disengaged, or absent employees.

Negativity hurts.

No matter how well-intentioned, negative actions in any form (thought, word, or deed) damage your business. It's like throwing oil on a fire. Is it a surprise that up to ninety percent of startups fail regardless of their potential?

To improve your odds, everyone on your team must quickly and appropriately take action when negativity appears. Unlike in mathematics, two negatives do not make a positive when people are involved. Your greatest asset will be learning how to use positive energy to limit and handle negativity.

**Positivity helps. It's not just nice to do—it's essential.**

When unhealthy stress pushes us to act, our woman entrepreneur may impulsively want to:

1) punch something or yell at someone (Fight)

2) run away from it all (Flight)

3) stop caring and collapse into a catatonic state. (Turn off the light/shut down)

+)  Or display more subtle clues where negativity causes harm.

These familiar choices rely on survival-mode thinking, where stress is a threat. Like gravity, these forces are strong. It takes strength and discipline to resist.

**Survival-mode thinking destroys our chances for success.**

Once I realized I had to make better choices under stress, I discovered the power of mental toughness. It became easier to be more authentic and build stronger relationships.

**Mental toughness is a skill that lasts a lifetime.**

Mentally Tough Women (MTW) know how to achieve more at every step of their journey. They enjoy what's next—no matter what's ahead. The speed at which they recover from the unexpected is determined by their skill set. The trick is to keep stress from stealing your best efforts and turn what others see as their worst moments into real success stories.

When you constantly train and prepare for contingencies, each time you're knocked down, you come back stronger and smarter. With good timing and the support of key people, I altered years of tradition that previously held women back. When I led a $2.1B engineer command in combat, stress and I were allies.

**Stress is your ally, not your enemy.**

Nothing great has ever been achieved without dreaming big and taking risks to make it happen. Yet many people mistakenly see all stress as something to avoid or eliminate. Imagine what's possible once you see stress as your superpower, allowing it to help you achieve more than ever before. Throughout history, mentally tough women have given us much of what we enjoy today.

MTW example. This modern-day Wonder Woman, supported by a gifted and unified global network, continues to inspire millions. Watch the official recording of Beyoncé singing "I was Here" for World Humanitarian Day, August 19, 2012 (https://youtu.be/i41qWJ6QjPI).

Beyoncé's a gifted singer who's strong, confident in her abilities (see how she stands), fierce, compassionate, and fun. And she's a wife and mother. Clearly, she's a master at handling stress. She also got there through hard work, tough lessons, and setbacks that fuel her success.

**MTW use positive stress to propel them forward and upward**

MTW understand that negativity triggers unhealthy stress in every form—mental, physical, and emotional. MTW know how to keep unhealthy stress from stealing their best and threatening their well-being. They anticipate and respond well to their environment. Much as river rocks are smoothed as they tumble in the current, MTW understand that life experiences shape who we are. We have a choice in how we view every experience and how to handle it.

MTW strive to be A.W.E.S.O.M.E. like the Goddess Athena, Wonder Woman, Beyoncé, and mere mortals like you and me.

**A:** Amazing, always give your best, be adventurous, ambitious, aloha spirited, always authentic

**W:** Wisely communicate (like Athena—ask better questions). What matters most? What are your options? What is there to learn? What is there to do?

**E:** Elemental—the power and energy of earth, wind, fire, water—eager, extreme, ever-changing and always the same

**S:** Safe and Strong—use all the tools in your armory—Helmet (apply Wisdom), Shield (Protection from negativity), Sword (Deflect direct attacks)

**O:** Observe to Assess and Understand—optimistic when looking for dynamics, trends, clues, snapshots, harmony, pono (good/not good) through a positive lens that keeps options open

**M:** Make it happen—mastery, mentor, manage, motivate, maintain the peace and harmony, make everything and everyone pono (good)

**E:** Every experience shapes who you are today—easy/hard or +/- or ups/downs, energizes and fuels your awesomeness

**Powerful MTW Tool.** Here's one you'll love that my clients find life-changing and part of a five-step training program on How to Handle Extreme Stress—my special gift to you.

**Your Ten Second Reset.** Unhealthy stress shows up where? Our breathing. Any restriction starves us of oxygen, throws us into survival mode, and hijacks our wisdom. This may happen when you become nervous about giving a talk, have the urge to blow up at someone, or when running late to some event. Once aware, immediately start "The Waterfall Method."

Imagine a Hawaiian waterfall. Use your wonderfully engineered nose to breathe in three seconds of cool air, like the cool, clean waters of a waterfall. Visualize it powerfully cleansing your body of any negative baggage inside you. In the next seven seconds, picture any toxic thoughts or goo being flushed from your body as you push the hot air out through your mouth. How do you feel now? Under extreme stress, you may need multiple resets. With greater skill, one reset quickly helps you regain your best.

**As you hone your Mental Toughness skills, your choices improve, your relationships strengthen, and your successes multiply. Every day brings a sense of adventure and infinite possibilities.**

Army Colonel Deb Lewis graduated from the US Military Academy of West Point (est. 1802) in the first class with women and went on to serve another thirty years in the US Army Corps of Engineers. Colonel Deb led a $2.1 billion dollar reconstruction program in combat amidst bombs and bullets, a fifteen-percent monthly worker turnover, and explosions around her. She recently led the Veterans of Foreign Wars for the State of Hawaii with over 4200 members. Her book "Why Is Pono Not Pono Today?" helps families make better choices when stressed. Her 5000 students in 120+ countries are learning how to handle extreme stress and stress basics. A Harvard MBA and founder of Mentally Tough Women (www. MentallyToughWomen.com), Colonel Deb is considered one of the world's foremost coaches on stress management and mental toughness.

How To Handle Extreme Stress: Learn five steps to transform extreme stress and difficult situations into opportunities for greater success. When you follow these steps, you'll regularly achieve more than you can imagine.

www.MentallyToughWomen.com/hww-gift

*"The clothing you put on your back is an incredibly accurate indicator of what you think of yourself and your life."*
A. BAUMGARTNER

# The Perception of Success: The Art of Strategic Self-Presentation

## DEANNA DUPREE

There's no getting around it. In this world, you're better off being good-looking. At all ages, and in all walks of life, attractive people are judged more favorably, treated better, and cut more slack. Mothers give more affection to attractive babies. Teachers favor more attractive students and judge them as smarter. Attractive adults get paid more for their work and have better success in dating and mating. And juries are less likely to find attractive people guilty and recommend lighter punishments when they do. Wild, right?

Not all of us are born with good looks, but we can present ourselves in a way that still attracts the business connections and attention we desire.

I came across a staggering fact that suggests eighty-six percent of people (men & women) of ages twenty-one to eighty-one are more willing to give money to someone whose dress style resembles their own. Wow! With that in mind, I ask you—does your style of dress connect with your audience/peers?

The Art of Strategic Self-Presentation requires us to examine our audience and our non-verbal approach to how we do business. My question to you, my darling, is this: Who are you hoping to gain trust with? Who's sitting across the table? Who's scrolling your feeds, viewing your profile and website? What will grab their attention? What will evoke a "Hell yes! She's my person?"

These are questions to strongly consider before you get dressed for that meeting.

The more you learn about your audience, the better you can plan communication. By this I mean strategically self-present. By knowing and understanding your audience, you will have the ability to speak to them in terms of what matters to them, all the way down to their favorite colors, hobbies, pets, etc.

Here are just a few strategies to learn more about your prospective client/ audience:

## 1. PROPERLY DEFINE YOUR IDEAL CLIENT

You identify your best prospects once you have defined your best clients. This is often referred to as an "ideal client Profile", and it can help you define prospects with the greatest potential. Once you know what you are looking for, it is easier to identify a great prospect from across the room. You'll recognize key indicators from how she wears her hair, to the length of her dress, or color of her eyewear. It will all become crystal clear, and you two will become a magnet to one another.

## 2. DO YOUR HOMEWORK

Investigate your prospects before meeting with them. The best potential client is always a referral from a great customer. Get to know more about them through the lens of your trusted customer. Social media has made it so easy to stalk people. I'm kidding, but it's so true. You better believe me when I tell you the prospect is also investigating you, your website, your Facebook friends, your videos, and the like. You'll learn so much about their personality, beliefs, likes, dreams, values, and more. Use all your reconnaissance to strategically, and stylishly, prepare for the Magnificent Meet.

## 3. ARTICULATE YOUR VALUE WITHOUT SAYING A WORD

A prospect with potential has a good idea of what they want and the need they are looking to fulfill. Humans have an innate desire to be led, inspired, and motivated. We want to know our money is in good hands. We want to feel confident that our service-providers can and will get the job done. Consider this: whether hiring a contractor or the cable guy, we are instantly impressed by the cleanliness of the uniform, haircut, their timeliness, wit, knowledge, and ability to communicate effectively . . . are we not? The same is true for you, my dear! Your prospect should see (and feel) your confidence, your class, your charisma, and your ability to get the job done . . . from across the room. They will intently watch for, and analyze how the room responds to your presence, and your image—the outfit you're wearing, the color choice, your hairstyle, nail polish, shoes, your smile, your warmth . . . it's all building the concept of value. Whether you like it or not, that cha-ching is either ringing louder in their head, or dwindling with every unlikeable impression. Goddess, before walking out of your front door, or hitting that "go live" button, ask yourself: Does my image match my invoice? Am I in alignment with my brand, my messaging, or mission? If it's a "hell yes", by all means, please proceed.

Fun fact: lasting first impressions are eight percent of what we say, thirty-six percent of how we sound, and fifty-six percent about how we look!

From what I know to be true of personal style, clothing is a tool to convey whatever message or first impression we want to make—and also a tool used to feel comfortable and confident. The same thing is true of money. It's a tool to use for the things that matter to us most.

So how do we show up fashionably wealthy? Glad you asked, my dear. You're about to bear witness to The Art of Strategic Self-Presentation.

## IT'S CONFIDENCE - COLOR - CLARITY

The following four approaches are key to dressing with confidence, color, and clarity!

1. **Discover & Dress Your Body Type:** It's imperative to get comfortable with what looks good on your body shape. This happens by knowing and understanding every intricate detail and curve of your frame. Start by getting head-to-toe measurements. If you can't do this on your own, make an appointment with your local tailor, or Nordstrom stylist. They'll be happy to measure you and help identify your frame and best features. This is the first and fastest way to identify what works perfectly for your figure.

2. **Play Up Your Strengths:** If you have a curvier figure, you might be more commanding in a dress than a pantsuit, for example. If you are tall, vertical stripes will emphasize this, while horizontal stripes will do the opposite. Take a look at your features, like leg length versus torso length, or how wide your shoulders are, and take that into account with your body shape and colors. By knowing what's flattering to your shape, paired with choosing the perfect outfit—IN your power color—you will command the room in a well-coordinated ensemble, no matter your style!

3. **Know Your Comfort Level:** Nothing is worse than being in an outfit that makes you feel uncomfortable. It's okay if you're someone who likes to show more skin, but be aware of how much skin you're showing. If your dress is longer than you prefer, you might feel frumpy. On the other hand, if you prefer to cover up, a plunging neckline or a dress that's shorter when you sit might make you feel anxious. Consider how comfortable you are with what your outfit does or doesn't cover before you walk out the door and you will always feel confident in the way you're dressed.

4. **Playing with Color:** Depending on the setting you find yourself in, whether it's presenting your company's new strategic mission to the board or meeting with a supplier to address problems in their performance, choosing the right color to wear plays an immediate role in the way you are perceived. Below, you'll find a quick reference to The Business of Color.

## THE BUSINESS OF COLOR

As an entrepreneur wearing many hats, color may not be front of mind when developing your brand and marketing materials or preparing for a meeting. But for better or worse, color affects the way people react when they first encounter you. Color has a powerful subconscious effect on every part of our lives, without even saying a word. An understanding of the meaning of color in business gives us an invaluable tool to get the best response to our marketing and promotional efforts and ultimately to create a successful business.

The biggest deciding factor is knowing which colors look best with your complexion and hair color and are appropriate for your audience and the purpose of the meeting. My top five power colors:

- Gray: Evokes sophistication and neutrality. It can be used in a suit or a dress. It looks powerful, but not as dominant as black. Gray indicates analytical and logical thinking.

- Red: Transmits energy, passion, and leadership. It demands attention and controls the environment. Also known for strength and courage. However, it could also present anger, aggression, and rebellion. Ideally, use red as secondary styling elements such as with a scarf or tie, shoes, or lip color. Red is considered masculine. Pink, feminine.

- White: It is a good color for shirts and blouses. Conveys sincerity and simplicity, and adds a little shine without being too overwhelming. Indicates that the person is organized.

- Blue: Trust & responsibility. Helper. Rescuer. Nostalgic. Friend in need. It is sincere, reserved, and quiet, and doesn't like to make a fuss or draw attention. The person who wears blue hates confrontation and likes to do things in their own way. Blue sends a welcoming sign. It's great for first meetings. From a color psychology perspective, blue is reliable and responsible. This color exhibits an inner security and confidence.

- Black: Despite its popularity, black is a color that represents authority, power, and even drama. It is useful for law firms or senior executives, but it can be overwhelming in a relaxed working environment. Wear black when you want to exude strength, elegance, and excellence.

I realize I've given you a lot to consider in how to show up fully, while standing out stylishly. Follow these tips to guide your shopping excursions and for inspiration when preparing for a meeting.

Life Transformer, Girl Boss, Inspirational Speaker, Style Strategist, Femininity Influencer & Empowerment Coach? Who's that girl?

On a typical day, you'll find The Fabulous DeAnna DuPree, affectionately known as "America's Most Stylish Social Butterfly," shopping, styling, teaching, or planning when to shop, style, or teach.

Based in Scottsdale, Arizona, this trendsetting shopper helps influential entrepreneurs make bold first (and lasting) impressions with their wardrobe choices.

As a Life & Empowerment Coach, DeAnna's personal story of overcoming self-hate, self-sabotage, and brokenness gives her powerful insight into how to lead her clients into living an abundant life through embracing and unleashing their divine personal power and beauty. Through her Boss S.O.S.S. Program, and FLAWED Masterclass, DeAnna has successfully designed a transformational experience for her clients, rather than a mere shopping trip.

A savvy traveler and femininity influencer, DeAnna empowers overworked and undervalued women to Return to Eden™ and reawaken their divine feminine essence by retreating to a secluded location quarterly to reconnect with themselves, lean in, listen, and let go.

DeAnna is on a mission to enrich the lives of a million people worldwide. With her impeccable track record, she's well on her way.

Use this 7-video, two-page guide for expert advice on how to dress to manifest your dream career, clients, and crowning chap. Get my number one approach to creating an hourglass frame in two easy steps!

Walk away with clear and practical techniques to shave a few inches off of your waistline, appear leaner, more sophisticated, and brilliantly confident. Additional bonus: A downloadable Wardrobe Essentials checklist every Female Entrepreneur MUST HAVE. If you're ready to elevate your life by learning how to discover and elevate your personal style, download this gift, exclusive to the Business With A Woman's Touch community only. Value $297.

https://freegift4u.deannadupree.com/11-steps-to-discover-your-style

*"Vision is the art of seeing what's
invisible to others."*
JONATHAN SWIFT

# Hold Tight to Your Vision

## MARCIA K. MORGAN, PH.D.

Ah, the wisdom of the old Irish proverb, *If you don't know where you're going, any road will do.* Just imagine how bumpy and circuitous that ride would be. Isn't it better to have a clear vision of where you want to go and follow a straighter, more direct road? You'll make better time with fewer potholes and, ultimately, be happier.

Similarly, and travel metaphors aside, women who are successful have a clear vision for themselves and their business. They know where they want to go. They've taken the time to be mindful and purposeful in their endeavors.

What is your vision? What do you want to achieve both monetarily and personally in your business and in life? Have you thought about how to hold on to that vision over months and years? Research shows, if you are just in it for the money and there is no internal passion/emotion or sense of fulfillment, burnout is inevitable. Your vision slips through your grip.

Business schools often ignore the part of the vision process that many women embrace. Namely, how do you want to feel?

You are more likely to succeed when you have a vision that produces a positive emotional outcome. That good feeling helps you hang on tight.

Regularly monitoring your feelings—the glue that holds everything together—can help you move through the four steps to reaching your vision.

**Step 1: Identify the vision for your business.** Think big picture, identifying your dreams and aspirations, what you want things to *look* like and how you want to *feel*. If it brings you joy and happiness, it won't feel like work and you will stay the course. If both head and heart are intertwined in the vision, the more likely you will stick with it.

**Step 2: Create an action plan with incremental goals to get you to your vision.** The goals should be measurable, specific, clear, and on a timeline. It is like a to-do roadmap where you can see your progress and know if you are on the right track. Every goal gets you closer to the vision.

**Step 3: Find "goal objects."** A goal object is an item selected by the woman to represent or symbolize her goals. A small toy truck sitting on her nightstand symbolizes her plan to open a food truck. A tiny world globe sitting next to her computer symbolizes her desire to take her clothing company globally. A miniature stuffed dog dangling from her backpack symbolizes her desire to become a veterinarian.

Research shows if people are regularly *reminded* of their goal, they are more likely to achieve it. It keeps them focused and on task, working on their plan. Mindfulness and visualization can stimulate action. Goal objects are that reminder. They take the one-dimensional "vision board" concept to another level—the objects are tangible and touchable. They are not cut out of magazines, but are collected in purposeful guided steps—the collection process is part of the focus and motivation. They are also with you or in prominent locations to be seen every day.

**Step 4: Expect and anticipate setbacks.** Setbacks have the capacity to shake one to the core and loosen that "grip" of holding tightly to that vision. The most successful women see setbacks as temporary, expected, a learning opportunity to readjust and reset, and navigable. Setbacks are not personal nor permanent. If you change your mindset to see roadblocks and setbacks as learning opportunities and steppingstones to your goals, you are more likely to stay on track.

**Typical barriers, roadblocks, and setbacks women experience:**

- *Lack of Time, Energy, Planning* – Make space for and prioritize your goals. Even when you are busy, slow down the chaos/craziness and work on your goals. Set boundaries. If you lack energy, get to the source—do you need better sleep, more exercise, etc.?

- *Fear of Failure* – You fear you will fail, so you don't even try. Reframe your thinking: it is only a "temporary delayed success." Stretch yourself and endure discomfort so you can grow and gain confidence. Embrace, don't fear, the unknown.

- *Fear of Success* – You fear you'll be discovered as a fake or undeserving of success. Will your friends desert you if you succeed and are different from them? Will men avoid successful women as partners? (Would you really want a friend or partner like this who doesn't support your dreams?)

- *Fear of Looking Inward* – Self-examination can feel hard but rewarding. How do you start? What will you discover? Will the social equilibrium change if you change? Some women read self-help books while others seek a counselor or friend to facilitate the journey. The more you know about your strengths and weaknesses, the more you will be able to meet challenges.

- *Perfectionism* – The dreaded "P" word. Some women postpone making a decision or taking action because they think they aren't ready and the end result won't be perfect. How do you know unless you try? Who says it has to be perfect? Is there really a perfect time for anything? People need to experience failure in order to learn, become stronger, gain new skills and confidence. Life goes on. Don't let that little voice on your shoulder stop you from getting out there and trying.

- *Procrastination* – Start by asking yourself if you are a "waiter" or a "creator." Do you let life happen to you, or do you lean in and create the life you want? Do you respond to things to try to control fear and discomfort or go full-on towards your vision? There are many reasons women procrastinate: poor time management, creating busyness, passive-aggressive behaviors such as making someone wait for you, your goal is not a good fit or enjoyable, and fear. Drill down to find out why you are stuck. Chunk tasks into small, doable steps. Find support from a partner, coach, friend, or colleague. Get to your core passion—why did you want this vision in the first place? Do positive self-talk to get through it.

- *Sabotage By Self Or Others* – Your self-talk and behavior, as well as the actions of those around you, should support your efforts.

- *Trauma* – Past emotional or physical abuse can be stressful and impact self-esteem, concentration, and energy. Seek help from mental health professionals who can offer guidance.

- *Learned Helplessness* – "Victim thinking"; blaming others.

- *Lack of Self-Esteem* – Unsure you can really accomplish what you want. We all have doubts. Be your own cheerleader. Stay curious, be an advocate for yourself and your vision.

- *Fear of Risk-Taking/Discomfort Around Feeling Vulnerable* – Girls are raised to be less risk-taking than boys. Work through the discomfort and congratulate yourself when you accomplish little steps.

- *Impatience* – Some people have overnight success but most do not. Be steady, deliberative, flexible and keep your eye on your goals and vision.

Here are some tips on how to handle setbacks:

- **Take a break and get distance from the issue**. Restore yourself, get perspective, and recharge.

- **Be gentle on yourself.** Forgive, let go, and move forward. Blame and grudges are not constructive.

- **Conduct an analysis.** What happened? What were the lessons learned? You now know what didn't work (that is useful information!). Identify all the things you learned from this setback.

- **Review your original vision and goals.** Did the goal fail you, or was it the approach and circumstances that failed? Do the goals need to be tweaked?

- **Reinvent yourself.** If needed, create a new course of action. Let this temporary barrier be your fuel. What can you do differently?

- **Visualize success.** Get re-energized and reinvigorated by looking at your goal objects. Take time to daydream like you did as a child, with the same freshness and wonder you had lying on your back in the grass, staring up at the sky. Visualization helps spark creativity and get you back on track.

- **Jump back in.** Be open and receptive to new ways of doing things. Staying positive can illuminate paths you may not have noticed. Allow yourself to be a little vulnerable, ask for help, get a mentor, share ideas and needs with others. Stay open to where the process takes you.

Now that you have found a road to follow, go for it. Be prepared for your trip with your vision in one hand, your action-plan roadmap in the other, and goal objects to remind and motivate you to keep you moving forward.

Marcia K. Morgan, Ph.D., is the author of a book for women, *GO! How to Get Going and Achieve Your Goals and Dreams at Any Age.* She brings a wealth of experience helping women and girls reach their full potential and have a voice in all parts of their life. She draws on more than forty years as a national consultant, researcher, trainer, and author on gender and crime. She and her husband live in Bend, Oregon.

For more information and to see inspiring goal objects from other women, please go to my website https://marciakmorgan.com. You can also download a free questionnaire, "How Close am I to Reaching

My Goals?" This short quiz will help you assess your progress towards realizing your vision and goals.

Additionally, short, free YouTube coaching videos are available exclusively to readers of this book. Get more tips on how to stay motivated and keep your vision and goals in sight.

Video #1 - What is Your Vision?
https://www.youtube.com/watch?v=nZphq7iIKzY

Video #2 – Prioritizing Your Time
https://www.youtube.com/watch?v=D_AEk2-ffyg

Video #3 – Finding Your Goal Objects
https://www.youtube.com/watch?v=Fdd5pPrz3ig

Video #4 – Handling Setbacks and Challenges
https://youtu.be/LDimAQFbnjY;

Video #5 – Creating Action Steps
https://www.youtube.com/watch?v=Qw8CjgX1ybw

*"The intuitive mind is a sacred gift and the rational mind is a faithful servant. We have created society that honors the servant and has forgotten the gift."*
ALBERT EINSTEIN

# Using Your Intuition to Make Business Decisions

## MARILYN ALAURIA

Intuition is an incredible tool to use in business, particularly when combined with consciousness, intention, and decision-making.

The Oxford Dictionary defines intuition as the ability to understand something immediately, without the need for conscious reasoning.

Most people refer to intuition as following their gut. Or they just knew it was what they had to do. Intuition is a feeling, a deep knowing that you need to say *yes* or *no*.

By deciding to create a business, you activated that unconscious "mission" part of you and responded to your vision, aligned with your truth, and engaged your senses. Now you are ready to take action towards your goal. This deeper part of you (your intuition) knows what can help you succeed.

Learning how it works in your body and employing it on command is key. The more you know your body—your instrument—the more you will intuit if something is good or not.

Conscious reasoning can sometimes impede your most important decisions. Fear may be inhibiting you, or a bad experience or a negative belief is keeping you from your destiny. It's why you want to learn how to summon and rely on your intuition and use it with conscious thinking. Don't let conscious reasoning without awareness drive the decision-making ship.

When you are aware of what you are thinking and engaging your intuition, you can make informed decisions and lay a foundation for future decision-making processes. Your intuition may say no and your consciousness can remind you why it's a no. When they work together, you may not struggle with that decision again or you will see the red flag right away. Being conscious of your thoughts as you work with your intuition will help you succeed.

We all have the gift of intuition. Try to recall a time when you engaged your intuition. Maybe it was when you were deciding what school to go to, whether you should go on that date, buy that car, have dinner with friends. Something told you to do it or not and you listened, and it turned out well.

Maybe you disregarded your intuitive hit and went anyway, and while at the event, you felt annoyed with yourself for not listening. You wonder why you went against your intuition.

People often ask me why they don't listen to it. I often explain that is actually how you grow the muscle of intuition. By going against it, you learn how your intuition works with your body. You can recall the moment of deciding and remember what you felt in your body when you were deciding. Did you feel queasy in your gut, an anxiousness in your heart, or have sweaty palms? By remembering how your body was giving you the message, it will help you pay attention the next time you have to decide. Then recall your reasoning that pushed you to go against those feelings. Recall is your best tool when you want to build the muscle of intuition. Don't sit in the regret of what you didn't do. Let bad decisions guide you on what to do the next time around.

Our body knows the truth of what it is we desire. We forgot how to listen to it. People taught us at an early age to listen to others over ourselves. When we were young and had intuitive hits, people often disregarded us for having these feelings and told us we were wrong, so we believed others over our own intuition.

I teach people how to develop their innate gifts by showing them how to use their own instrument, their body, mind, and soul. Don't like the word soul? That is okay. Use whatever word speaks to you. Because no matter what belief system or spirituality you follow, you are intuitive. Get back to knowing when these feelings are happening, pay attention, trust them and act on them, then get caught up in semantics. Sometimes you won't know if you were right because nothing will go wrong, but I can promise you it will continue to take you toward your success because you will be deeply listening to your truth.

Intuition is extremely helpful when building and running a business. There are a variety of ways you can use it to save time and money.

It helps you identify potential opportunities that you may otherwise pass up. By listening to your inner guidance, you may notice something that is perfect for your market or where you want to take your business.

It helps you make decisions. When your heart is in your business, it's sometimes hard to know the right or wrong answer. Your intuition can help you make clear decisions—no matter how hard they are—that align with your values and vision.

It can help you hire people, let go of people, and build the right relationships. It will guide you to know who an excellent partner would be and how to cultivate potential referral relationships. By knowing how to use your intuition, you can tell if someone is being truthful or not and whether they will be a good fit.

Most importantly, it helps you to trust yourself. You will develop more confidence in your own abilities and grow the business that is right for you.

Once you learn how your intuition is communicating with you, it helps you to read the situation and how you feel about it and make powerful decisions. The more you trust yourself, the more confident you become about how you are running your business, which leads to greater success.

Developing intuition is a process that requires practice and self-awareness. Here are some ways you can work on your intuition:

Pay attention to your body. First, take a moment to think of a time you engaged your intuition or made a significant decision and it worked out for you.

Think back to that time and try to remember where you felt it in your body. Don't worry about getting it wrong. You can't. Use your imagination and allow yourself to pick a place you felt this information lived. Was it your heart? Your stomach? Your hands? Your big toe? It's different for everyone. No matter what, decide on an area where you feel your intuition lives.

Practice becoming conscious in the moment. Your increased awareness of negative, habitual fear thinking will save you years of making wrong decisions. One life changing tool I teach for getting conscious in the moment is by using an alarm. You can learn more about this technique for free here: https:// JoinSASS.com.

Before you make a big decision, pause and reflect on how you are feeling in your body. As you breathe, bring your attention to your breath and scan your body. What do you feel? Then, after you decide, repeat this and notice if your feelings have changed. Maybe you feel relieved or you are still nervous. Becoming aware before and after a decision will help you hone your intuitive skills.

You will also learn to trust yourself. As I take you through this next exercise, I ask that you completely trust yourself. Don't worry about getting it right or wrong. Just use your imagination and let yourself go. The more you work the tool of trust, the more confident you will grow in your intuition.

Think about something you absolutely love. The closest thing to unconditional love that you know. Once you have it, close your eyes, go to the part of your body you chose earlier, and feel that love. What color is in this area of your body? What color is that love? Don't see a color, then give it a color. Remember, I said you can't get it wrong.

Now think of something that really upsets you. Maybe it's a past decision or something someone said to you. Something you really hate or have a strong feeling of dislike towards. Now close your eyes, go back to that place in your body, feel that uncomfortable feeling, notice what color it is. Don't see a color, give it a color.

The first color is a yes, and the second color is your no. Your body is communicating with you, and you are communicating with your body. You are letting your intuition know you will listen. Work this muscle. Learning to work with your intuition is like working a muscle out in the gym. You don't get a sixpack with one crunch.

Practice taking things you love and reinforcing that color in that part of your body and do the same for things you don't love.

The next time you struggle with a decision, close your eyes, tap into that part of your body and see what color shows up. You now have your answer.

The more you practice using your intuition to guide you on your journey, the more successful you will be.

 Marilyn Alauria is a gifted psychic medium, teacher, and author of the book, "Guides: Mystical Connections with Soul Guides and Divine Teachers." She has an unmatched capacity to ignite deep, soul-level transformation for her clients around the world. As the creator of Next Level Living and Soul Finder Academy, she has given us a clear action plan for developing our talents, following our purpose, fulfilling our dreams, and living in alignment with our souls. She simplifies the path to living a life of peace, ease, and alignment, making true fulfillment easy and achievable for her students.

After a successful, Emmy Award-winning career in the entertainment industry with MTV and NBC Olympics, Marilyn shifted her focus to sharing her natural gifts and helping others discover their own intuitive abilities.

You can learn more about Marilyn at MarilynAlauria.com or on her podcast "Who Can It Be Now", wherever you listen to your favorite podcasts.

Negative beliefs that are buried deep inside of you can derail your dreams and invite chaotic living. The first S in the SASS Pillar system is about SUBCONSCIOUS AWARENESS. Take this powerful technique and shift your unconscious thoughts for good.

Https://JoinSASS.com The 4-pillar system taking you from positive thinking, remembering who you truly are, igniting your passion and living in synchronicity.

*"It is unlimited what the universe can bring, when you under-*
*stand the great secret, that thoughts become things."*
FEARLESS SOUL

# Finding Emotional Support

## NANCY MUELLER

**W**hen you're looking for emotional support, you're usually looking for a way to feel better and YOU are the only person who has the power to make you feel anything!

Emotions are energy in motion: energy + motion = emotions.

The Universe as we know it, see it, and experience it, is not all there is. The Universe is always in motion—it's a vibrating, pulsating, magnetizing force. At the molecular level, everything is in motion, including you!

The pure formless substance of the Universe—whether you think of it in spiritual terms such as God, Higher Power, Spirit, or the Universe, or address it mentally as Infinite Intelligence, Universal Mind, or the area of quantum physics—is known as the field of all possibilities. This power—however you perceive it—is the source of everything you desire.

The Universe is always awaiting your recognition and will create, attract, and guide you based on your emotions and how you're feeling. This is The Law of Attraction, which is a universal law. Like the laws of physics, chemistry, gravity, and mathematics, the Law of Attraction never changes.

Everything that exists is energy, including you, your thoughts, your feelings, and your emotions.

Because everything is energy and your energy field is pure consciousness, it has an innate knowing. This means your inner consciousness knows why you're looking for emotional support and will guide you to it if you allow that to happen. You can think of your innate knowing as your Inner GPS.

When you're looking for emotional support, your inner guidance will take you places based on how you feel. If you're feeling positive, you will attract people, places, and experiences that create feelings of positivity and when you're feeling negative, your inner guidance will attract people, places, and experiences to support your negative feelings.

Positive emotional support can raise your negative feelings (vibrations) based on your emotions when you ask. Many people sit in meditation or prayer asking for something, or for their life to be different than it is, from a place of emotional pain. But remember; you are a walking, talking, thinking, acting Being of vibration—you are energy in motion! All energy vibrates and all vibrations attract similar vibrations.

Simply stated, emotions are the result of all your experiences. The moment you recall an experience, whether it's a negative experience or a positive experience, and whether it's happening now or in the past, how you feel about that experience creates your state of being.

When you're looking for emotional support, you are looking for a way to feel better.

When you need emotional support, it's often difficult to see your gifts and your talents because you're holding on to a negative or limiting belief. A belief is a thought you think over and over again until you've created a story based on what you're thinking and feeling. If your story is negative, what you think about, talk about, and tell others about, will cause you to feel negative emotions and feelings within your body. Everything you keep bottled up inside of you builds momentum. The question you must ask yourself is, "Do I want that momentum to explode in happiness or struggle?"

We all have free will. You can choose to suffer in silence, or you can choose to free your mind by going beyond your story to let go of the negative emotions it's creating.

The first question to ask yourself is, "What's my story?"

What is the story you're thinking and telling yourself and others about your past or your current struggle or experience? Why are you telling this story? How does thinking about, or telling your story make you feel? Why does your story make you feel this way? Are you ready to go beyond this story? Why or why not?

It doesn't matter how often something happened, or how big a role this experience played in your life. When you focus on it, you attract more of the same. If your story doesn't feel good, you're setting yourself up for mental, physical, and emotional struggles.

Are you beginning to see how your story is responsible for the emotions you feel in your body? When you're in a mindset of negativity and you want to turn your negatives into positives, start by concentrating on something that makes you happy or brings you joy.

As soon as you become aware of the negative story you're telling yourself, or saying and sharing with others, choose a pivot word. A pivot word is one word you can use as a trigger to remind yourself your thoughts, feelings, and emotions are going in a direction you don't want them to go. Choose a word that is silly or nonsensical and has nothing to do with your current situation. As your mind focuses on your pivot word, think about something that makes you happy or brings you joy. You only need to hold onto a better feeling thought for sixteen seconds for your emotions to shift from negative to positive. Once you feel the shift, hold it for another sixteen seconds and another and another until you feel your mood lift. This helps you go beyond your story to receive the emotional support you're looking for.

Feeling guilty about wanting to express sadness, guilt, fear, anger, blame, or shame only means you are holding those negative emotions inside you. Allowing yourself to express what you're thinking and being honest about how you're really feeling gives you the power to let go of your negative story. You don't have to carry the experiences of the past around with you. If you do, it only keeps you from enjoying who you are in the present moment.

When looking for emotional support, the first question to ask yourself is, "What do I want to feel better about? What is weighing me down in mind, body, and spirit that is causing me to look for support?" Your answer is creating your story about why your life isn't going the way you'd like it to go.

Your inner GPS can give you all the emotional support you're looking for as it guides you to shift from negative to positive. Something in your life must shift in order for you to take the next step, and if you choose not to shift, you'll find yourself looking for emotional support in all the wrong places.

None of this information will do you any good unless you apply what you've learned and make it a daily practice. Knowledge isn't power—applied knowledge is power. Practice going beyond your negative stories until you have mastered this practice. When you've mastered going beyond your story, the emotional support you're looking for will be readily available to you.

Whether this information is new to you or a reminder of what's possible, there's too much information available today to dismiss this work as woo-woo, too far out, or impossible. You may have difficulty believing it, but that only means you're telling yourself a story about what you're capable of. Your negative stories create your desire for emotional support.

Your mind is full of stories, but they're not only your stories. You've also created beliefs around the stories taught by your parents, grandparents, and generations before them. There's a lot of shifting, sorting, and sifting needed when you go beyond your personal story.

Everything you've learned and believed up to this present moment has kept you safe or supported your life's journey. Honor your resilience and allow yourself to practice this new perspective until you are able to pull from it without thought. Mastering something means you've learned to make it part of your daily habit and have done the necessary work to be able to draw on it whenever you require emotional support and guidance.

As you repeat this process when other stories come up, you'll immediately recognize your triggers. You'll know where these messages come from and how to work to neutralize your triggers. You will have mastered your beliefs to go beyond any story that could pull you out of alignment with your inner being.

Like gravity, the Law of Attraction is always working, whether you know it or not, whether you understand it or not, and whether you believe it or not.

Everything in this chapter can be backed up by science. As science and spirituality continue to find common ground, what used to be referred to as woo-woo is now seen as solid science.

Your mind is like a library full of stories. Some of them are supporting your dreams and desires and some of them are squashing your dreams and desires.

I am here to remind you that it's not what happens to you that matters, it's what you do with what happens.

As the founder of Mastering Your Beliefs, clients usually refer to me as their "Sensei" a title from my days as a student, competitor, and teacher in the martial arts.

Martial arts taught me my strongest weapon is not my physical strength, it's my inner strength—the power of my mind.

A childhood of secrets that included mental abuse, verbal abuse, and physical abuse that escalated to sexual abuse by the age of twelve set me on the path to heal my inner child.

My path to mastering my beliefs started the minute I chose to stop believing that being victimized made me a victim. Nancy Mueller ~ Life Sensei

Manifesting our desires happens more easily when we're feeling positive vibrations! Download this FREE video tutorial on how you can turn your negative feelings and beliefs into positive feelings and beliefs in four easy steps. https://www.masteringyourbeliefs.com/

*"Procrastination is the art of keeping up with yesterday and avoiding today."*
ATTRIBUTED TO WAYNE DYER

# How to Stop Stalling Now!

## WENDY PAQUETTE

We, as humans, get to admit stalling can be one of the most frustrating and demotivating experiences not only as an entrepreneur but as a beautiful, powerful human. Whether we're struggling to make progress on a project, grappling with a difficult decision, or facing a creative block, stalling can leave us feeling stuck and uninspired. Right?

Fear not, lovely, there are steps you can take to get unstuck and start moving forward again. Let's begin by identifying when and why we stall.

Let me ask you a few questions first to get us into the aligned headspace to see if this information will serve you in the best way. Feel free to write your answers down. They may trigger something new. Ready?

**Question #1:**. When you notice you are stalling, at what point of time is it in the process? For example, a day later, halfway to a deadline, a day before it's due?

**Question #2:** What emotions come up for you when you notice the stalling happening?

**Question #3:** What steps do you then take to end the stalling and get going?

Don't fret, these questions are just to get your mind in the right space to understand that stalling is an indicator that identifies limiting programming that is holding you back from your desired result.

What do I mean by limiting programming? Well, throughout our lives we initiate mental programming, also known as belief systems, that in a powerful way become the template for how we choose our next steps consciously or unconsciously. Next steps that ultimately form our experiences and our life, like it or not.

These belief systems can be installed at a young age or, actually, anytime we decide what is true for us based on our experiences. These experiences cause us to formulate a belief around what certain things mean about us, about our lives, and about others. These belief systems become the cornerstone of our lives, creating the hue of the lens through which we view and experience the world.

Unfortunately, many of these decisions that create belief systems (or mental programing) do not serve us in the manner we would like. Ultimately, they can create some frustrating and limiting blocks that prevent us from having everything we would like in this life—and this includes money, relationships, even health.

Blocks create the experience of stalling.

If you believe in divine timing, kismet, magic, or quite frankly even if none of these are a part of your thinking, you have decided to read this book. Because of this, you now hold in the palm of your hands not only solid business advice from wonderful authors, but the ability to change everything that has been holding you back.

Following are ways to identify your potential limiting belief systems that directly get in the way of the things you want and that create that frustrating experience of stalling.

## HOW TO IDENTIFY YOUR LIMITING BELIEF SYSTEMS THE MOMENT YOU NOTICE YOU ARE STALLING

We are going to assume you have noticed you are stalling on a project or a decision. What happens next is a practice that will serve you for the rest of your life. Ready? Read and reread this carefully.

What emotions come up for you the moment you realize you are not choosing to do the one (or multiple) thing that is on your to-do list? What will help get you to your next step or next level?

Let me help you with some examples of LBS or what's known as a limiting belief system:

- Thoughts such as "I'm clearly not good enough."

- Thoughts about worthlessness: "What's wrong with me?"

- Feelings of not being deserving or feeling angry. "Why do I keep forgetting about this task?"

- The feeling that you're mentally lacking, or forgetful.

- Feeling dumb, mindless, incapable, nervous, fearful, anxious.

You get the idea.

Now take some time to address a moment when this is real for you and identify the emotions that come up. If you believe no emotions come up, I would invite you to take the time to really be in the moment for this. We are really good at hiding our true feelings, especially from ourselves. Set a timer for five minutes and see what you can come up with.

Got your list of emotions? Wonderful! Now let's celebrate! Congratulations, you have taken a huge and powerful step to get on your way to stop the stalling the moment it starts.

This first step is critical for understanding *why* you stall in the first place and what is in the way, so you can stop stalling all together. I'm not suggesting we are perfect in any way, as perfection is one of the emotions that often comes up when stalling is happening, but I am suggesting that once you are capable of identifying when you are stalling and the appropriate emotion that comes up, you will become more resilient than ever.

Imagine moving at lightning speed when you can address those pesky limiting belief systems that get in your way and sneakily cause you to not move forward on your path to joy and success.

Now that you have identified that you have emotions that come up, the next step is to address these emotions in whatever way you can in order to stop them in their tracks. They indicate the presence of the belief system that is creating an actual pause in your steps to success. These emotions (and all emotions essentially) are what make the experience of being human so wonderfully unique. When you can embrace your emotions and allow them to become a partner to your understanding of how you function in the world and be the key to opening up the gateway to limitless success and amazing experiences, you raise your potential for ultimate success.

To conclude, stalling can be a major obstacle for us humans, and sometimes can be even more frustrating for entrepreneurs. But by identifying its source, aka limiting programming or belief systems, we can quickly identify and minimize stalling and start making progress.

Remember, progress, not perfection, is the key to success.

Wendy Paquette is the personal advisor and confidant to the world's elite creators.

She helps them remove the mental programs holding them back so they can actualize their deepest desires. She does this using a technique she pioneered and refined over the last 10 years, called multi-dimensional timeline shifting.

As a result, her clients are able to access Self-Actualization and their peace paradigm with extreme clarity, achieving limitless visionary successes in life and business.

If you would like to accelerate this process to identifying your limiting beliefs and blocks so that you can have everything you want, create the momentum that accelerates the life of your dreams with peace and ease, you may book an assessment call with me to see if we are a great match to get you to your next

level. Here is the link, https://wendypaquette.as.me/WOMANSTOUCH. To connect with me via social media, you can find me on my website: https://wendypaquette.com/

As a valued reader of this book, I have a free gift for you—my workshop on how to identify your limiting belief systems. You can find your gift here: https://wendyp.live/WomansTouchGift

This three-hour workshop is a powerful, hands-on pre-recorded experience where you get to learn and understand from a unique perspective how to identify your limiting belief systems so your view of your current reality shifts to support you.

# the
# FOUNDATION

*"A brand for a company is like a reputation for a person. You earn reputation by trying to do hard things well."*
JEFF BEZOS

# The Anatomy of a Visual Brand

AMANDA GOFF

Most business owners are familiar with the need to formulate a business plan, marketing plan, and elements like the color pallet or logo. But what is often not given as much careful consideration is what the brand stands for and how its story should be translated visually. This mistake in the brand development process can create a gap between the written (or spoken) messaging and the visual messaging, which could cause confusion or even be subconsciously off-putting to potential clients. This is why developing a visual brand is vital to a brand's success.

So, what exactly is a visual brand and why is this so important?

A visual brand is one that taps into the brand foundation (core values, mission, vision, voice, key messages, and brand personality) and uses this to develop the brand's visual identity. The foundation should serve as the support structure of brand communication and helps ensure consistency across all platforms or collateral. An intentionally designed visual identity should shape how a brand's story is told (marketing plan) and gives the tools to connect with those ideal clients from the time they get their first impression (growth plan).

It is important to have a strong visual brand because it helps to create an emotional connection with your ideal client and establish trust. Additionally, it can help to differentiate you from your competitors and give your business a professional, polished look.

To break this down a bit and explain it further, I created this quirky overview that I call the "Anatomy of a Visual Brand." This, paired with the companion workbook, can be used to assess a current brand, or give an edge to one being developed.

**Bones of Your Brand:** This is the foundation and the elements that make up a brand's story. Just like the bones of the body, these elements are underneath it all and provide structure. Everything listed below contributes to developing a brand's message and building the visuals to tell your story.

- Ideal Client/Audience/Client Avatars

- Core Values

- The "Why" Statement

- Mission/Vision

- The Unique Solutions Provided

- What Sets Your Brand Apart

**The Nerves:** This is the inner process that connects information throughout the brand and shapes how the brand communicates. If this is not functioning properly, a misfire can cause confusion or misguided action. The nerves of a brand are made up of the brand's personality and brand voice. Both of these, using marketing psychology, contribute heavily to selecting the color pallet and font.

**The Personality:** The set of human characteristics associated with a brand. It is the way a brand acts, looks, and the attitude it evokes. It can be used to create an emotional connection with customers.

**The Voice:** A brand voice is the distinct choice of words and tone used in communication. It should reflect the brand's values, mission, the "why" behind the brand, and the overall message. A brand's voice should be consistent across all communication channels and be tailored to the audience it is trying to reach.

**The Muscles:** This is the strength in a brand and what will do the work to tell a brand's story in a dynamic way. The visual elements create that "thing" that is unique to your business, helping you stand out, and building brand recognition. It is critical that the "muscles" be connected closely with the "bones" and "nerves" to know how to show up. Your visual elements need to work together with your story (foundation), personality, and voice to communicate the same message.

- Color Pallet: Look at the psychology and theory of all the color choices. Color is a powerful tool and will subconsciously impact the message desired for a brand.

- Font Choices: Just like color, the type of font used communicates a visual message.

- Images or Video: Regardless of how these are used in marketing, a picture is truly worth a thousand words. The chosen style, voice, and topic (yes a brand possesses these) will impact the effectiveness of these tools.

- Graphics: Think about the iconic graphics of popular brands. Why do these stick in your mind? This, of course, includes the logo, however, there are many other graphic elements that can serve as visual "muscles."

**The Brain:** This is the how, where, and how often (aka . . . The Visual Brand Plan). This tethers to the marketing plan and should include a more overall strategy for visibility. The "brain" helps to create a common vision for the brand's marketing efforts, sets measurable goals, and identifies the most effective methods for reaching those goals. A successful plan and strategy should also include a plan for tracking the success and return on investment (ROI) of the marketing efforts. This will help a brand refine and adjust the strategy as needed to be effective while staying authentic, relevant, and grounded in the brand foundation.

**The Heart:** This is the person (or team) behind the brand. Why should you share the people behind the brand? Because people are curious and knowing what is behind a brand is fascinating. Sharing the who, the why, and the story is what resonates with an audience. By introducing the people who are responsible for the product or service, people can see the brand in a more personal and relatable way and create a sense of community. The audience will start to recognize the faces and feel like they are part of the brand's story. Just as the heart pumps blood that feeds the rest of your body, those behind the brand should be flowing into the brand as a whole.

**The Skin:** This is the attraction factor when all the visuals come together, and the consistent presence is intentionally crafted to share a brand with the world. Just like our skin, this is the first thing that is experienced and can make or break a brand. This can be online, in print, or in person, and this is where consistency is king. Be certain you know how you are showing up, even though a brand is not just skin-deep. A good way to get an idea is to perform a digital brand audit.

In today's digital age, having a strong visual brand is essential for businesses to stand out from the competition and create a lasting impression on their customers. A visual brand serves as a guide for businesses to show up consistently across all their marketing channels, making it easier for them to build brand recognition and trust with their audience. It can also create an attraction factor with your ideal clients. When customers see a brand that looks professional and cohesive, they're more likely to trust that brand and consider purchasing from them. Creating a strong visual brand is not just about making things look pretty, it's about providing the clarity needed to confidently tell your brand's story.

Overall, a strong visual brand is an essential tool for businesses looking to succeed in today's crowded marketplace. By investing in a cohesive and consistent visual brand, businesses can build trust, create emotional connections, and attract their ideal clients. So, if you haven't already, now is the time to make sure your visual brand is working hard for you.

Amanda is one of the rare ones who practices in the field she went to school for. As head visual ninja at Silver Keys Media, Amanda gets to work with creatively minded entrepreneurs to help them attract the clients they want to work with through visual marketing. She specializes in helping business owners unlock their brand's story and tell that story visually through images and video. She strongly believes in the power of collaboration to make things happen and brings to the table her experience as an actor, director, filmmaker, photographer, and her 15+ years in marketing.

Some of her "street creds" include: A Bachelor of Arts in Broadcast Communication and Theater; She co-directed and produced the local indie films "Unmarked" and "Legend of the Forest", and she is a nationally published photographer. When not having fun with her clients, Amanda loves spending time playing games or hiking with her son and daughter-in-law. She is also a theater geek and indie filmmaker and loves getting into creative mischief with her friends.

As a business owner or entrepreneur, it is more important than ever to have a strong visual brand. With the rise of social media and the number of places to show up, businesses are competing in a crowded marketplace, and it's essential to stand out from the competition. A strong visual brand can help a brand achieve this by creating a unique identity that resonates with its ideal audience.

The "Anatomy of a Visual Brand" workbook gives you an opportunity to look at what you have already going on, where you can strengthen your brand, and how you can improve the way you are showing up.

This exercise will cover your brand foundation, the elements that make up your story, what is your brand's personality and voice . . . and so much more. https://thepublishingcircle.com/Amanda

*"The first responsibility of a leader is to define reality. The last
is to say thank you. In between, the leader is a servant."*
MAX DEPREE

# Evolutionary Leadership:

## The Benefits of Unlocking Inner Genius And Allowing Your Team To Be The Leader They Already Are
### VICKIE HELM

I n the corporate world, leadership has often been equated with a set of characteristics or traits that are embodied by a single person at the top of an organization. This traditional model of leadership has been challenged by the concept of evolutionary leadership, which recognizes that leadership is a process that emerges from the collective efforts of a team. By unlocking the inner genius of each team member and allowing them to be the leader they already are, organizations can experience a range of benefits, including increased innovation, greater employee engagement, and improved performance, as well as better job satisfaction.

To understand the power of evolutionary leadership, let me tell you about my friend Alex, the CEO of a fast-growing tech startup. Alex is a brilliant engineer who had founded the company with a handful of like-minded individuals, and they had enjoyed rapid success in the years since its inception. However, as the company grew, Alex found himself struggling to keep up with the demands of leadership. He felt like he was constantly putting out fires, and he couldn't seem to find the time to focus on strategic planning or product development.

One day, Alex attended a leadership seminar where he heard about the concept of evolutionary leadership. He was intrigued by the idea that he didn't have to be the sole leader of the company, and that by tapping into the collective intelligence of his team, he could achieve even greater success. Alex decided to try an experiment. He called a meeting with his team and announced that he was stepping back from his role as CEO, and he wanted each member of the team to step up and take on a leadership role in their area of expertise.

At first, there was some confusion and apprehension among the team members. They were used to looking to Alex for guidance and direction, and they weren't sure how to take on leadership roles themselves. But as they began to explore their individual strengths and passions, they started to feel a sense of empowerment and ownership over their work. This took a bit of time, but soon the team started seeing ways to improve the efficiency in their area of expertise.

One team member, Sarah, had always been passionate about user-experience design, but she had never felt like her ideas were valued or heard. With the encouragement of the team, Sarah began to take the lead on redesigning the company's flagship product. She conducted user research, prototyped new designs, and led cross-functional teams to bring her vision to life. The resulting product was a huge success. That one shift in product design raised profits by sixty-two percent, and it was clear to everyone on the team that Sarah's leadership had been a critical factor in its development and deployment.

Another team member, Tom, had always been interested in sales and marketing, but he had never had the opportunity to take on a leadership role in those areas. With the support of the team, Tom began to experiment with new marketing strategies and sales approaches. He collaborated with other team members to create compelling content, and he led a team of sales reps to pitch the company's products to potential customers. As a result, the company saw a significant increase in revenue, and Tom's leadership was credited with driving that success.

As each team member took on a leadership role, Alex found himself with more time to focus on strategic planning and product development. He was able to step back and let the team take the lead, knowing they were each bringing their unique skills and perspectives to the table. And because the team was more engaged and empowered, they were able to generate new ideas and innovations that Alex had never even considered. This experiment breathed new life into his company and its culture.

This is the power of evolutionary leadership. By unlocking the inner genius of each team member and allowing them to be the leader they already are, organizations can tap into a collective intelligence that is greater than the sum of its parts. This approach to leadership recognizes that leadership is not a position or a set of traits but is instead a process that emerges from the dynamic interactions of a group of people.

What are the benefits of evolutionary leadership? Here are just a few:

**Increased Innovation:** When each team member is empowered to take a leadership role in their area of expertise, they are more likely to come up with new ideas and innovations. By tapping into the collective intelligence of the team, organizations can generate more creative solutions to complex problems.

For example, as Sarah took the lead on redesigning the company's flagship product, she was able to bring her unique perspective and expertise to the project. She conducted user research and used her design skills to create a product that was more user-friendly and intuitive. Without her leadership, the company may have missed out on this innovative approach.

**Greater Employee Engagement:** When team members feel empowered and valued, they are more engaged in their work. By allowing each team member to take on a leadership role, organizations can foster a culture of ownership and accountability. This can lead to higher levels of job satisfaction and lower turnover rates.

As Tom took on a leadership role in sales and marketing, he was able to bring his passion for these areas to the forefront. He collaborated with other team members and led a team of sales reps to drive revenue growth. This sense of ownership and responsibility helped him feel more engaged in his work and more committed to the company's success.

**Improved Performance:** When each team member is able to contribute their unique skills and expertise, the team as a whole is more likely to achieve its goals. By unlocking the inner genius of each team member, organizations can improve their overall performance and achieve greater success.

As each team member took on a leadership role, Alex had more time to focus on strategic planning and product development. With the team driving innovation and growth, the company was able to achieve greater success than ever before. Alex told me he never expected to have such a powerful result and that he actually had been sleeping better at night because he wasn't trying to be everything to everyone.

Instead, he simply empowered others. He told me he'd learned that to delegate didn't mean looking over shoulders as people work, but instead it meant creating an office environment that values creativity.

He now does something I regard as genius. He has a technique he calls "tapping talent." When he has an issue or something he would like feedback on, he taps his team's talent to get solutions.

Evolutionary leadership is a powerful approach to leadership that recognizes that leadership is a process that emerges from the collective efforts of a team.

By unlocking the inner genius of each team member and allowing them to be the leader they already are, organizations can tap into a collective intelligence that is greater than the sum of its parts. This approach to leadership can lead to increased innovation, greater employee engagement, and improved performance. As Alex learned, sometimes the best way to lead is to step back and let your team take the helm.

Over the last three decades Vickie has built thirteen successful businesses, authored over forty books, spoken on stages around the world, and helped thousands of people grow more assets and wealth.

Her mission is to inspire twenty million business owners and entrepreneurs to live their inner genius and become wealthy, high-performance individuals.

She is the founder and CEO of Helm Media and Publishing, the leading digital publishing company for online visibility marketing.

She mentors and teaches the Freedom Seeker's Way Program with her business partner, Tracy Wilson, where they help entrepreneurial women CEOs scale or build their impact with an online company, influence, and revenues. https://freedomseekhersway.com/

She and her team of writers produce the weekly Precisionist Life Newsletter, delivered every Sunday for people who are or want to become high-performance individuals. Get your free newsletter at
https://precisionistlife.beehiiv.com/subscribe

Get your free copy of The She Myth here:
https://thepublishingcircle.com/SheMyth

*"I've learned that people will forget what you said, people will forget what you did, but people will never forget how you made them feel."*
MAYA ANGELOU

# The Journey of Your Next Customer Starts with a Single Step

### AMY BIDDLE

A customer is a person who buys something.

The people who will become your customers come from the millions of people you don't know yet.

It doesn't matter if you sell a product or a service.

Everything you do . . .

every product description you write,

every ad you run,

every video you produce,

every email you send.

Each of these communications needs to talk directly to your people.

And you need to say exactly what they want to hear.

And you need to say it at the time they're ready to hear it.

And you need to reach these people in the way they want you to reach them.

And you need to reach millions of people because there is so much competition online.

But don't worry. It's an impossible task that you can master.

## HOW ON EARTH DO I MEET MILLIONS OF PEOPLE?

These days, reaching new people has gotten to be terribly complex and expensive. But I have good news.

You only have to be marginally good at finding your people because so many businesses are so bad at it.

By focusing on your people first, you will win the race.

Introducing the Fuzzy Bear Sock Company. We'll use this successful and completely made-up company as an example.

The world has gotten much smaller since the birth of the commercial internet. We can reach people around the world whenever we want. And visitors can find us whenever they want. Printed mail marketing was never this fast. Nor was it ever this easy.

You can reach people down the street as easily as you can reach people in other countries.

But the smaller the world gets, the noisier it has gotten.

Realize this: you don't need to access the entire world. Nor would you want to. There isn't a need for Fuzzy Bear Socks to sell everywhere. FBS can be a multi-million-dollar business focused on the U.S. market alone.

Ten years ago, sellers could make a simple website and make quick sales.

They didn't need a lot of words or fancy tricks.

## SHOPPERS ARE MORE SOPHISTICATED NOW.
Fuzzy Bear Socks can't just show a picture of a neato pair of socks with a brightly colored "shop now" button next to it.

They need to describe the socks.

Visitors need to be able to imagine wearing the socks, virtually.

They need to actually sell the socks.

I could write an entire book about promo messaging, so I won't tackle that topic here.

The copy and video scripts have to reach out of the computer and grab people who will buy.

We can reach millions of people a day online. It doesn't cost too terribly much to do so.

Fuzzy Bear Socks only needs to sell socks to the people in the marketplace who want them.

The challenge is finding the right people.

And by focusing on the people first, FBS has become masterful at business.

The people who might one day buy from you could be people who don't know they need you.

Yet.

Or they might be people who know they need you but don't know about you.

Take the stance that your prospects know they have a problem they need to solve. Or teach people that they have a problem.

See the differences?

Those are different kinds of messages. Design each message to reach your prospects in different ways.

There are basically two kinds of audiences.

The first audience is what's called "cold."

Let's call these cold people "audiences."

Cold audiences aren't customers yet. They're prospects . . . prospective customers. They might even be suspects . . . you might suspect they could be customers at some point.

These are people who've never heard of you. It's also possible that these people don't even understand what you're selling.

The second category of prospective customers is "warm" audiences.

These are people who have heard of you before. Maybe they don't remember hearing about you. Remember, it's noisy out there.

The idea of the customer journey is deceiving.

You'd think it means a person goes from hearing of you, hearing of you again, and buying from you.

A customer journey has a beginning, middle, and end—sort of.

But there are a bazillion pits of snakes and burning trash piles between each stop.

Let's zoom in on how this works and take a closer look.

Brenda is thumbing through her Instagram, enjoying baby panda videos and makeup tutorials when she spots an ad from Fuzzy Bear Socks.

Brenda isn't thinking about socks. She isn't even shopping. But something about your ad caught her eye, so she shares it with her sister and moves on.

In the customer journey idea, Brenda is at the very beginning of the story. Coldest of the cold prospects.

But when she liked that Fuzzy Bear Socks' ad, she stepped up.

She got a little warmer when she engaged with the ad by sending it to her sister.

There are digital tools, called pixels, that we use to track Brenda's interest in Fuzzy Bear Socks. Because she engaged with the ad, we can find her again.

How these pixels work is outside the scope of this article. (But keep reading because I have a wonderful gift for you so you can learn so much more about tracking your customers online.)

Pixels let us use information we gather about Brenda so we can get in front of her again and again.

This is the first part of the customer journey.

Brenda discovered Fuzzy Bear Socks.

Brenda noticed Fuzzy Bear Socks again a few more times that day.

Then she bought.

I promise you, 99% of the time, that journey is not a straight line.

Brenda's customer journey looks like the path of the princess in an old-fashioned fairy tale.

She'll wander from her home and get lost in a forest where there are scary monsters (in the form of your competitors).

She'll fall in a well (losing her job).

She'll get captured by goblins (maxing out her credit card).

She'll look at over 547 websites (each page shows various ads for socks and other kinds of fun, work-from-home couture).

And finally, one day, as she's browsing the internet, the clouds in the dark sky part. The sun shines through. Today she is shopping. Today she needs to buy a gift for a friend.

Today is the day Brenda buys her first pair of Fuzzy Bear Socks.

I hear angels singing. Don't you?

Brenda bought! So we get to celebrate. But not for long. Because the story of Brenda's customer journey has actually just begun.

Now we have to get back to work.

Fuzzy Bear Socks can now reach her in so many more ways than most of their competitors can.

Most of those "other" sock companies didn't capture Brenda's email before she purchased from them.

And if they did capture her email, most of them don't do effective email marketing.

But now, after that first purchase, Fuzzy Bear Socks has the marketing trifecta. The hat trick. Now they have Brenda's email, her postal address, and her phone number. (Assuming their shopping cart has captured these bits of gold.)

After Brenda bought her first pair of Fuzzy Bear Socks, the next part of the customer journey began.

The next phase of the journey is no less harrowing than the first part.

It costs less to sell things to existing customers than it costs to find new customers, so it's far more profitable to sell a customer something else. Plus, it's easier to find them.

We assume that Fuzzy Bear Socks treats their customers like they are gold.

Customers get:

- their best stuff
- their fastest responses
- their earliest notifications

They can segment their customer list into various bits.

For example, they know everyone who bought the Fuzzy Bear Socks Northern Chill 3-Pack.

Do you think these customers will buy more? You can sell them the next set in the product lineup: the Winter Frost 3-Pack.

They only have enough socks to last a few days. So VIP customers can only buy three of these sets of three.

From their customer list, they know who purchased the Northern Chill 3-Pack. They know who purchased the small, medium, or large.

FBS can completely sell out of Winter Frost by sending emails, mailing postcards, or calling the people on the phone who already own Northern Chill.

Less expense means more profit.

More profit can go to more inventory, more support, and to the growth of the business.

Know who you want your customers to be.

Make the first sale.

Treat those customers like the gold they are to make repeat sales.

Do this process better than your competitors.

"It doesn't matter if you call what I do "fractional CMO" or "business consultant". I work with businesses to identify gaps and build the strategy and efficiencies to span those gaps." Amy Biddle is the host of Traffic Handler Podcast.

"I'm a strong believer in using tech and old-fashioned relationship connections to do good business. And yes . . . this can scale."

"You can get help with this entire process with a gift I have for you. The eBook, "eCommerce Business Transformation Guide" is a $96 value. But I want you to have it for free.

"I want you to understand one thing: Out of all the support I've ever created and provided to clients . . . something I can recommend to anyone with an ecommerce business . . . this one is the best. Hands down.

"Because no matter what you do, no matter what you sell, master the art of selling. Build wealth by growing the lifetime value of every single customer you ever serve. Doing this will serve you in every part of your life. Forever. What you'll learn in this book won't take enormous amounts of time to implement. You'll spend about twenty minutes reading. And you will spend less than ten hours a month implementing. All of this with the end toward doubling (or better) your store revenues in the next six months." https://traffichandlers.co/guide

*"If you don't concentrate on counting the money, people soon realize that money is not the focus of your consciousness, so they give you everything other than money: kudos, acclaim, praise, etc., etc. And sooner or later you'll be in trouble."*
STUART WILDE

# The Real Money in Life You Lose is the Money You Fail to Earn

CHELLIE CAMPBELL

J ennifer was at the top of her game. A successful business owner in the legal field, she was in high demand for her services, and regularly flew all over the country, consulting with her many clients. She was also a brilliant artist who wanted more time for her creative expression. She began consulting with me to make sure she achieved her current goal: to fully express all her creativity and earn as much as she could before she retired in a few years.

During one session, I asked, "When was the last time you raised your fees? What's the going rate in your industry these days?"

Taken aback, she replied, "Why, I don't know. I do know it's been a long time since I raised my rates."

"I suggest you ask some of your colleagues who do what you do and find out what people are charging these days. And figure out when was the last time you gave yourself a raise."

She called me a week later to report: "The going rate in my industry these days is $550 per hour. I've been charging $350 per hour, and I haven't raised my prices in nine years."

When she immediately raised her prices, she said there wasn't one whimper about it from anyone—neither her clients nor prospective clients.

I'm delighted that she is now earning about $200 more per hour and that's helping her accelerate her savings goals. But how much money has she lost in the last nine years by not keeping current with the market price for her services? How much further along towards retirement would she be now?

Here are my top three suggestions for negotiating for more money:

## 1. RESEARCH HOW MUCH MONEY IS AVAILABLE AND ASK FOR IT.

Here's an example from my book, *The Wealthy Spirit*:

Sally's eyes were snapping, and her face burned with resentment. "I've been working for these people for five years and have done wonders for them, but they are so stingy they are only giving me a three percent raise!" She was so hot she could barely sit in her chair.

It was a beautiful spring day, and we were sitting outdoors at the local restaurant. I knew something was wrong the minute she arrived. Sally was the Executive Director of the Chamber of Commerce and was quite visible in the community. She did a wonderful job, and I had seen the growth in the membership and programs of the Chamber during her tenure. I had no idea she wasn't well paid.

"Tell me everything," I said, "but start at the beginning. How long have you been working in this job?"

"Five years," she exclaimed, "starting as a part-time secretary. I've been full time for the past four years and have taken on many more duties and responsibilities. I've tripled their membership and their budget, but they still only give me tiny annual cost-of-living raises based on my starting salary as a secretary!"

She was seething.

"I'm going to quit!"

"Take a deep breath and relax a minute," I coached. "You can always quit—that's a last resort option. But you like the job, except for the low pay, so why don't we work together to try to get you the money you deserve?" She thought about that for a minute, then agreed it couldn't hurt to try.

Over the next couple of weeks, I coached Sally on how to get a raise.

First, I told her to lose the resentment—anger doesn't sell. People just get defensive. Not being well paid was her responsibility and hers alone. She had been waiting for the Board of Directors to recognize her contributions and voluntarily significantly raise her salary.

But she had not given them the facts and figures they needed to justify the increase.

Now she understood, so she put together a presentation for the board that outlined every achievement and the dollar amounts her contributions had made to the bottom line of the organization. She did her research and discovered the pay rates for the same position at similar organizations. She prepared written comparisons of the Chamber budgets for the five years she had been working for them.

We met again at lunch just before her presentation to the board so she could practice her delivery. "You haven't been paying me enough money!" she started out, and I stopped her.

"No resentment, remember? It would have been nice if they had thought you should be paid more based on the job you have done, but you weren't asking for more, so they thought you were happy. Try it again—be nice, be charming, and be strong at the same time."

She did a masterful job. She got a thirty-five percent raise in salary. We celebrated together that day.

Think about your own situation—what are your talents and skills really worth?

## 2. NOT CHARGING ENOUGH CAN DRIVE AWAY AS MANY CUSTOMERS AS CHARGING TOO MUCH

Years ago, a friend of mine decided to go into business for herself doing computer consulting. She told me she had a man who promised to send her a lot of business, so she called him up to tell him she was ready.

"What are you going to charge?" he asked.

"$40 per hour," she replied hesitantly.

"Then I can't send you any business," he stated.

"Why?" she asked. "Is that too much?"

"No," he replied, "it's too little. Any computer consultant worth anything is charging $100 per hour and up. I can't ruin my reputation by referring people to someone who only charges $40. Everyone will think you aren't any good."

You can do yourself irreparable harm if you charge less than market prices because people won't think you're good enough. Find out about the going rates in your profession.

## 3. PLAY THIS GAME TO CONVINCE YOURSELF YOU'RE WORTH MORE MONEY

A music composer named Steve had two goals in my workshop: 1) He wanted to find a new agent; and 2) he wanted to make more money.

After a few weeks, he came to class and proudly announced that he had gotten a new agent.

We all cheered and congratulated him, and then he said, "But I'm probably never going to work again now."

"What?" I said, "Steve, what are you talking about?"

He said, "I make $150,000 to score a film. My new agent wants to charge $200,000. I just don't think I can get that much money."

"Aren't there films with budgets of $200,000, $500,000 and even millions?" I asked. "Like John Williams who did *Star Wars*?"

"Well, of course there are," he said immediately. "If you're John Williams."

I said that John Williams didn't start out as a famous composer, he worked his way up. Steve needed to convince himself he was worth more, so I made up this game: He should take the amount he wanted to be worth—$200,000—and double it to $400,000. Then he should say, "I am paid $400,000 per film, I am paid $400,000 per film," twenty times per day for the next week. He needed to say it with positive emotion and intention behind it until he believed it.

117

Steve laughed, but he agreed to try.

At the next class session, I asked him if he had practiced stating his new price. He answered that he had, and it felt good. "How does $200,000 per picture sound now?" I asked.

"It doesn't sound like enough!" he answered, which provoked gales of laughter from his classmates.

How often do we restrict our reality to lower levels of possibility by not asking for enough?

I love this quote by Obediah Thomas: "Always ask for more. More than you think they will offer. More than they do offer. More than you made last time. More than you would settle for. More than you think others are charging."

You're worth more than you think.

Ask for it!

 Chellie Campbell wrote *The Wealthy Spirit: Daily Affirmations for Financial Stress Reduction* and two other books while teaching people about manifesting money and happiness for over thirty years. She is one of Marci Shimoff's "Happy 100" in her NYT bestseller *Happy for No Reason* and contributed stories to Jack Canfield and Gaye Hendrick's books. She was voted "Most Inspirational Speaker" by Women in Management and "Speaker of the Year" by the Association of Women Entrepreneurs. Helping people make more money and have more fun is her life mission!

My gift to you: Absolutely Amazing Abundance Affirmations!

These are my favorite abundance affirmations to say each day. Repeat them first thing in the morning, when waiting in line, driving, exercising, etc. Do them consistently for twenty-one days and you will have established a new prosperity consciousness habit!

You'll find the sign-up form at the top of the Home page at www.chellie.com

The Wealthy Spirit

Daily Affirmations for Financial Stress Reduction

Chellie Campbell

*"Financial freedom is available to those who learn about it and work for it."*
ROBERT KIYOSAKI

# How To Prepare Your Finances for Business Ownership

DANIELLE HARMON

Starting a business is exciting. It's a time of learning, growing, and seeing your dreams fulfilled. But the excitement alone will not lead to a positive outcome. Often, it's the personal finances of the business owner that lead to the stagnation or eventual failure of a business. In order to see lasting success, business owners need healthy finances. If you prepare financially for business ownership, then you will have a much better chance of substantial business growth and achieving your long-term personal wealth goals.

## WHAT ARE MY PERSONAL FINANCES, AND WHY DOES IT MATTER?

You want to create a firm financial foundation prior to launching a business, so it's important to know that your personal finances are organized and healthy. Your personal finances include anything you earn, own, or owe. It includes all incoming money, all outgoing expenses, and any assets you own, such as your home or other property. Debt or money owed to someone else is also included in your personal finances. If you have major financial issues, such as substantial debt or expenses substantially higher than your income, it will be difficult to sustain a new business.

## HOW TO GET STARTED
### Track Personal Expenses

Organizing your personal finances is the first step in preparing your finances for business ownership. Few things will provide more motivation in business than awareness of your personal expenses. It is essential that you know where your money is going, which requires tracking the money moving in and out of your bank account.

Start by creating a list of your monthly expenses and break down the list into two categories: discretionary and non-discretionary spending. Discretionary spending is dining out, entertainment, monthly subscription services, personal care, or other items that are not essential for daily living. Non-discretionary expenses are housing, utilities, vehicle costs, groceries, and other essential costs. As you compile the list of expenses, be sure to include costs that are paid quarterly or annually, such as insurance or membership dues.

With this comprehensive list of expenses complete, you are now aware of your current spending. The next step is to evaluate where you can make changes and establish limits that are realistic for your income level. Most importantly, do not let your expenses surpass your income level. The goal is to simplify or reduce any extravagant or unnecessary costs. Remember that determining where to spend your money is a trade-off. Either you can use it towards lifestyle expenses or you can use it towards future goals. Make the conscious decision to curb your spending in order to have money to use towards your business goals.

Once you have reviewed the list of expenses, you can establish an annual budget. The annual budget will outline all expenses throughout the year in various frequencies, including monthly, quarterly, and annually. The budget provides insight into spending patterns and seasons when your costs are more concentrated, such as at year-end. It will allow you to prepare year-round, encouraging you to be mindful of your expense timing and to prepare accordingly. Having success also means being disciplined to stick with it. Many people find it helpful to use a banking app or online budgeting software to track their expenses regularly.

## EMERGENCY FUND PROTECTION

With a budget in place, the next area of preparation is establishing an emergency fund. An emergency fund is an essential part of having the freedom to enjoy your business. The goal of an emergency fund is to cover unforeseen expenses and prevent the use of credit cards. Any unanticipated costs have the potential to derail your financial foundation if you are not adequately prepared.

While the recommended size of your emergency fund can vary based on each individual's situation, general guidelines suggest having enough cash reserves to cover three to six months of personal living expenses. A single income home would need a larger reserve or emergency fund than a dual-income household.

Calculate your needs below:

My monthly (personal) expenses are: _____

The cost of my personal expenses over a 3-month period is:

3 months * _____ = _____

The cost of my personal expenses over a 6-month period is:

6 months * _____ = _____

Your suggested emergency fund balance should be a minimum of the three-month number calculated above. If you are single, consider the six-month number your minimum. The larger your emergency fund, the more flexibility you will have with your expenses. It will also provide a bigger cash cushion if your business income is less than anticipated.

## DEBT: GET IT UNDER CONTROL

After your budget is set and your emergency fund established, your next step is to get your debt under control. Having debt creates a lot of stress and forces you to need a higher income. By eliminating your debt and subsequent debt payments, it reduces the amount of income you will need to bring in during the early stages of your business.

You want to create margin for the early days of business when sales will most likely be lower, otherwise it will be especially challenging to move forward with a business when the obstacle of large personal debt stands in your way. Avoid putting expenses on credit cards during this time. While it can seem like a convenient solution now, there is no guarantee of future income. Instead, use your emergency fund to help with extra expenses. Avoid getting buried in credit card debt and you will avoid major financial stress.

In order to take control of your debt, you will need to create a strategy. Start with the Debt Snowball approach, which is simple, yet effective:

**Step 1:** Create a list of your debts. Include the outstanding balance, interest rate, and time remaining to pay down the loan (if applicable).

**Step 2:** Organize your debts from the smallest to largest outstanding balance.

**Step 3:** Allocate the minimum payments to all debts. Then, starting at the top of the list, pay down your smallest debt first using your excess income. Be intentional in order to pay down the debt quickly. Once the first debt is paid in full, take the money previously used to pay off the small debt and put it towards the second debt. Work down the list until everything is paid off. Tip: keep your list in a visible location to remind you to stay the course and review your progress periodically.

**Step 4:** Celebrate your success!

Once your personal debts are eliminated, your financial foundation is very strong. No debt means you will be in a great financial position for business ownership and it will allow you more freedom with your income.

## BUSINESS FINANCIALS

Now that you have organized your personal finances, you want to do the same for your business finances. Start by creating a budget for your business. You'll want to conduct research to determine the costs you can expect. Know what expenses are reasonable compared to others in your industry and keep in mind how you can simplify or reduce costs.

If you anticipate especially high costs or inventory purchases, you need to be keenly aware of those necessary costs. As you are getting your business off the ground, it is important to consider if you can cover expenses with your emergency fund until you have steady, reliable income from the business. Starting with a sizeable emergency fund will prevent stress while building your business.

## KEEP THINGS CLEAN

A fundamental practice for a financially healthy business is to keep your personal expenses separate from your business expenses. Keep separate bank accounts for each, using your business account for business expenses and your personal account only for personal expenses. Tracking these items separately has an impact on many areas, including taxes.

## 3 TIPS FOR SUCCESS

1. Keep it simple! You want to know your expenses, but you don't have to track every single dollar. It doesn't need to be perfect.

2. Be informed! The goal is to be aware of where you are right now. Maybe you aren't where you want to be, but now you know how to get there.

3. Keep moving forward! Don't be discouraged when it doesn't happen overnight. Gain knowledge and make changes over time.

Building a business can be financially rewarding, but in order to set yourself up for great financial achievements, you need a solid foundation. This foundation consists of organizing your expenses, establishing a sufficient emergency fund, and eliminating your debts. These three practices applied both personally and professionally will place you in the perfect position to enjoy financial success. Use the free resources I'm providing to make sure you're financially prepared for business ownership.

Danielle Harmon, CFP®, is the founder of Boundless Financial Services, LLC, a fee-only financial planning firm providing comprehensive financial planning services to busy entrepreneurs.

Her career in finance began more than sixteen years ago when she started working with a large, regional broker-dealer. From there, Danielle worked as a trader and back-office operations associate with a newly formed, local broker-dealer. As she gained experience working on financial plans, Danielle worked for several independent RIA firms as a Paraplanner and Associate Advisor.

Danielle has a B.S. degree in Finance from Oral Roberts University. She has been a Certified Financial Planner™ Professional since 2017. She formerly held the Series 7 and 66 licenses and the SC Insurance License.

Danielle is a native of upstate South Carolina and resides there with her husband and their three sons. When she's not crunching numbers and working on financial plans, you can find her spending time outdoors with her family.

**Quickstart Guide: 4 Easy Steps to Prepare Financially for Business Ownership** Everyone wants a strong start to their entrepreneurial journey. In this guide, you'll find worksheets and quick tips to help you get started. Once complete, you'll be organized and well on your way to a solid financial foundation.

QUICKSTART GUIDE

Get Your Finances Organized in 4 Easy Steps

https://mailchi.mp/15b5d2052b08/financial-quickstart-guide

*"I follow three rules: Do the right thing, do the best you can, and always show people you care."*
LOU HOLTZ, AMERICAN FOOTBALL COACH

# Creating a Fantastic Culture for Employees

### DEB BOELKES

A s you learned in an earlier chapter, crafting a magical brand is vitally important for your business to thrive. Creating a fantastic culture that enlivens your magical brand is beyond important as you begin to add employees and scale your business. To attract, hire, and retain the very best people, consider how you'll create a Best Place to Work culture well before you start to interview potential team members.

Workplace culture is the culmination of what people do, how they do it, and why they do it. Culture is comprised of the values the team lives by; your communication style and the way you treat people—from your staff to your customers and your vendors—the traits and actions for which you want your business to be known; and so on. At the end of the day, your culture is everything that makes your business unique and difficult to emulate. The culture your business manifests will determine how people experience and value your brand.

To create a fantastic culture, it's essential for everyone on your team to find purpose and meaning in their role. It's difficult for potential employees to get excited about your organization if they don't understand your objectives and the core principles that set you apart from your competition. It will be impossible for you to align each individual's vision of personal success with your business vision of success if your mission, vision, and values are not crystal clear and meaningful to them. Therefore, your first step should be to clearly define the mission, vision, and values of your business.

One Fortune 150 company where I worked for nearly a decade initially lured me in when a good friend who worked there suggested I would relate well to their values and vision. I had the opportunity to meet the CEO/Chairman on my first day of leadership orientation. The CEO/Chairman was clearly passionate about the company and all it stood for, and he quickly captured the hearts and minds of each of us with the special way he made us feel like cherished members of his family. His mission—and now our mission—was to foster this kind of passion in everyone reporting to us. I instantly knew I belonged there.

I will never forget his closing remarks: "With every decision you make, think about the potential ramifications. What if your decision ends up as the cover story in the national news? Would your mother be proud to see it? If your decision won't make your mom proud, then think again." Of course, no one wants to disappoint their mother, and we knew we would never want to disappoint him, either.

To maintain a fantastic culture, your most important responsibility will be to enable each team member to be the best they can be, doing whatever it is they truly love and want to do. After years of mentoring "high potentials", I came to understand just how many people don't really enjoy their jobs. While some will begrudgingly hang on because the money is good, anyone who doesn't enjoy their job will not likely ever meet your—or their own, or their peers', or your customers'—performance expectations. Lackluster performance of your team will be your downfall, so stay vigilant for any telltale signs.

Whenever I've asked an unhappy employee or mentee, "If you could wave your magic wand and do something else, something you would really love to do, what would that job look like?" I often found their answers somewhat surprising. Their dream job often bore little resemblance to their current role—hence, their lackluster performance. Redefining someone's responsibilities to better align with their personal desires can result in a magical transformation, both for the individual and for the business. So never hesitate to take such actions.

I always made a point of developing close, trusting relationships with everyone on my team. My objective was to ensure each person was on a path toward achieving their own vision of personal success—in alignment with our business vision, of course. Then I would hold each team member accountable for high performance.

When interviewing potential employees, be sure to have those "magic wand" discussions right up front to ensure they will be a good cultural fit. Then stay observant for any indications of faltering performance as you add staff, because even your best performers can quickly become demotivated when others around them are disgruntled or allowed to slack off. I learned early on that taking swift corrective action was always the right thing to do if I detected anything a little off kilter.

Thanks to having those "magic wand" discussions whenever warranted, I rarely found it necessary to put anyone on a Performance Improvement Plan—although I never hesitated to do so when necessary. After discussing their situation and exploring the options, the underperformer would either get their act together, or I would help them proactively move on to something more in line with their passions and desires. In the end, the entire team would thank me, even the underperformer.

As a result, my teams virtually always exceeded objectives. We had tremendous camaraderie, and highly motivated career seekers wanted to be part of our fantastic culture. My standard practice was to keep a steady stream of pre-qualified high-potential superstars waiting in the wings to immediately fill any openings that occasionally occurred. It's truly amazing how a high-performance culture attracts high performers.

Keep in mind that your team members are always observing you as their role model, just as young children observe and mimic their elders. It's up to you to set the stage and make your culture as welcoming and engaging as possible. Establish and maintain high performance and behavioral standards and be the kind of role model everyone *should* emulate. Let your own WOW shine and your workplace will shine along with you.

I'll share an example. The owner and head chef of one of my favorite breakfast cafes never fails to delight because she goes out of her way to make everyone feel special. She treats every customer and every member of her staff as if they are her dearest friends who she is always excited and blessed to see. She keeps a big smile on her face that grows even brighter whenever someone new walks in the door.

This ever-cheerful business owner loves to share her passion for the business and she's always quick to show how much she appreciates and values every member of her team. As she tells it, "Running this business is never a chore. It's a joy!"

For this reason, potential employees and customers alike are drawn into the place like magnets. Her enthusiasm brightens everyone's day, and the café consistently receives high ratings and reviews on social media and in local magazines. This business owner is the epitome of a role model Best Place to Work entrepreneur. Just imagine how vibrant your workplace might be if you adopted practices and a demeanor like hers.

As you scale your business, make ongoing mentoring a daily activity or you'll miss the opportunity to build the kind of close, trusting bonds that can enhance your culture. Make a habit of chatting with your direct reports every day, whether in person, by phone, or via Zoom—to keep in touch and find out if there are any new roadblocks that you might help eliminate.

If team members only hear from you every now and then—when problems arise at your end—they'll begin to perceive you as the bearer of bad news. They'll want to avoid hearing from you. With friendly, caring, and helpful conversations each day, however brief, instead of being perceived as a superior who sits in judgement—on a mission to point out faults—your insights and opinions will be sought out and welcomed. You'll be positioned to nurture and grow enthusiastic disciples, and you'll be perceived as the valuable mentor you should be.

I certainly cherished all the close-knit moments my team members and I shared over the years. No matter how brief our daily chats may have been, everyone was comfortable candidly sharing concerns as well as any crazy, out-of-the-box ideas they may have had to move the business forward. Even when my team members were half a world away, we all felt a close bond and looked forward to our conversations. Our culture became the flagship of our industry.

Creating a fantastic culture for employees is really quite simple if you and your team:

- Keep your mission, vision, and values top of mind.

- Define and maintain high performance expectations.

- Love what you do.

- And take pleasure and pride in creating WOW together.

All you need to do is start where you are, give your team the best you have to give, expect the same in return, and together strive to make yours a Best Place to Work culture.

**Deb Boelkes** is the award-winning author of *The WOW Factor Workplace: How to Create a Best Place to Work Culture, Heartfelt Leadership: How to Capture the Top Spot and Keep on Soaring,* and *Women on Top: What's Keeping You From Executive Leadership?* and her latest book, *Strong Suit: Leadership Success Secrets From Women on Top.*

Having spent thirty years climbing the career ladder within male-dominated Fortune 500 technology firms, Deb knows firsthand the challenges women can face in their efforts to reach the top. That's why in 2009 she founded the leadership development firm Business World Rising (originally called Business Women Rising) to accelerate the advancement of high-potential women and men to the top of "Best Place to Work" organizations.

In *The WOW Factor Workplace,* Deb changed our expectations about achieving joy and fulfillment from our jobs. In *Heartfelt Leadership,* she changed our expectations of those who lead. *Women on Top* transformed the way women pursue their careers and *Strong Suit* provides the candid mentoring every woman needs to become the best leader she can be on her way to the top.

Deb speaks to corporations, industry associations, and universities the world over—both on stage and as a podcast guest expert—on career advancement, leadership development, and creating "Best Place to Work" organizations. She is regularly featured in publications ranging from *CNN Business* and *Thrive Global* to *Authority Magazine, Diversity MBA Magazine, Advancing Women,* and industry-centric periodicals like *Women Leading Travel and Hospitality.*

Deb received her bachelor's degree in business administration and her MBA in management information systems from the University of Rhode Island. She lives on Amelia Island in northeast Florida with her husband, Chris. Together they have three grown sons and four granddaughters.

**10 Introspective Questions to Ask Yourself Today**

To help you get started creating a fantastic culture for employees, Deb Boelkes has a **free gift** for you: **"10 Introspective Questions to Ask Yourself."** Download this free gift at https://www.businessworldrising.com/creating-culture

# the
# TACTICS

*"Authenticity, living your truth, kindness—*
*these are necessary virtues."*
MERLE DANDRIDGE

# Elevating Your Engagement

## MOLLY MAHONEY

**W**hat if you could create social media posts that inspired loads of engagement from your ideal clients and leave the members of your community begging for more?

As you may have guessed: You can!

Let's start with a story.

Before I was a human connection and AI-obsessed social selling strategist . . . As a young performer hitting the NYC audition scene, I found myself falling lower and lower as I went into audition after audition without actually landing a job. I was like countless other young actresses who pour their heart and soul into their dreams: wide eyed, bursting with talent, and hungry to please.

Then it all shifted.

I went to what is called an Equity Chorus Call (ECC), an audition where members of the Actors Equity Association (a union for stage actors), are guaranteed a chance to audition for a spot in a performance. At the time of this audition, however, I was not a union member. I was trapped with the other budding performers in a long narrow hall outside of the audition lounge. Surrounded by women who were taller, thinner, younger, older, just . . . "er" than me.

There were times that these auditions would last all day: literally, eight hours spent sitting on the floor or a little bench trying to stay fresh for the two-minute make-or-break moment of your life, ending with a simple, "I'm sorry we won't have time to see you today."

Are you kidding me?

No, I'm not.

This particular day we had all been waiting for about three hours when I needed to use the restroom. I went to the woman at the front desk and muttered politely, "Excuse me, where would I find the restroom?" The woman at the desk looked at me, raised one eyebrow and said, "If you go downstairs, out the front door and to the right, you'll find a McDonalds in Times Square."

Uhhh . . . what!?

"I'm sorry?" I said, "I'm here for the audition."

"Do you have an Equity Card?" she replied.

"No, but I'm here to audition." I smiled.

"If you don't have an Equity Card, you can go to the McDonald's in Times Square," she reiterated with a straight face.

I turned around and stared into the faces of twenty to thirty young, desperate girls, picked up my giant bag, which held my jazz shoes, tap shoes, character heels, audition book filled with sheet music and headshot/resumes and food for the day because I'd be trapped in the hallway, and went back to my 400-square-foot apartment.

What ON EARTH was I doing with my life? Spending endless hours waiting for a two-minute shot at a job? Walking into a room *begging* for the chance to be seen? I walked down those stairs and knew something had to change.

And it needed to change NOW.

What was it that was stopping me from booking work? From being seen in these auditions? Suddenly, it all became clear.

When walking into these auditions, I was trying to impress, trying to be what they needed in their production, trying to guess what they were looking for and doing everything possible to be just that. I was doing everything possible to do the impossible. There was only one thing I could be more of that would actually improve my shot at booking a show.

Maybe you've found yourself in a position like this. Maybe you have wondered why you aren't finding the success you know you deserve, knowing that you have worked tirelessly to achieve a promotion or a goal or a feeling of success and freedom—and yet, you are still sitting in that narrow hallway, using the restroom at possibly the shadiest spot in Manhattan, unable to break through.

There is one thing that you can bring with you that will change your feelings of doubt and change the way you are affecting the "casting directors" in your life. That thing? It's *you*.

Yep! **YOU** are the secret to your success.

Not just the you who is begging for the job or promotion or newfound freedom in life. YOU who are FILLED with an unbelievably unique sense of awesome.

Before you start to challenge me or start throwing out "yeah butz", I want to be very clear. Everyone has something that makes them uniquely awesome, even if it's just the fact that they make an amazing quesadilla.

I needed to STOP trying to be what "they" wanted in auditions and be more of what I already was. I made a concerted effort to spend every day celebrating what made me awesome, what filled me with joy (my own quesadilla recipe) AND searching out and celebrating what makes others uniquely amazing as well. And do you know what happened? I started booking work like a madwoman. I earned my union card, and booked show after show, including a National Tour and a long stint at a regional theater that eventually brought me to my husband.

You can do this too! If you firmly commit to unlocking and celebrating what makes you awesome, you'll find the same shift in your life.

Start by making a list. A list of ALL the things that make you awesome. If it's hard at first, don't worry. This is an ongoing list to which you can keep adding. These can be character traits that you possess, and also things that give you that bubbly feeling in your chest that fills you with joy.

**Here's a guide to get you started:**
Skill Sets

Activities
Appearance
Values
Things You Like to Eat

As you head into each day, each meeting, each situation, those are the things that you should lead with.

No, you don't need to walk into a room and say, "Hi! I'm Susan and I love Brussel sprouts!"

But you might want to look over that list and recall the way Brussel sprouts make you feel . . .

Or maybe your quesadilla of awesome is made up of knitting, or skiing, or helping others. Once you've connected with your awesomeness, bring those things to the front of your energy, hold them in your chest, and beam them out like rays of sunshine.

Then—and this is the best part, with EVERY person you meet—recognize that there are things that make them equally awesome.

They have their own quesadilla recipe that fills their chest with bubbles. They may not be aware of it yet, but if you can focus on finding their quesadilla and celebrating it, the energy in the room will shift. You'll draw in others who have more in common with you, allowing you to connect in business and in personal relationships. And you will stop comparing yourself. By celebrating their awesomeness, you will give your inner glow a chance to burn a little brighter.

Okay, now . . . what does that have to do with upping your "engagement" for your business?

EVERYTHING!

Discovering YOUR AWESOME is the first step in our three-part social media engagement system.

We call it The Social Triangle™. This is the foundational key to unlocking the algorithm of your chosen platform, letting you generate more sales with less content. (And hardly any calls.)

There are three components to the triangle:

1. You

2. Your client.

3. The platform you choose to use

. . . and that juicy intersection of those components is where the magic happens.

Now, let's dive into each one of these a little more.

YOU: You need to show up and actually exist on a platform. Lots of businesses opt to do this purely via ads; while this can work, we prefer the approach of, you know, being a human.

Who woulda thunk it?

Putting in the effort to be authentically YOU will go a very long way. And . . . it's honestly RARE.

YOUR CLIENT: Know who they are and be where they are. We call these Awareness Playgrounds. When you identify where your client is spending time, and YOU show up there too, the algorithm will notice, connect the dots, and put your content in front of the RIGHT people who are a great fit for your products and services.

THE PLATFORM: Give the platform what they want. Keeping people engaged and staying on the platform for a longer period of time means more time for the platform to show them ads, meaning the algorithm will prioritize your content.

When these three pieces come together, MAGIC IS UNLOCKED!

Keeping the principles of the Social Triangle™ near and dear to the heart of your business gives you the tools to build and maintain your own Social Selling Circle™.

If you aren't quite sure about the power behind this strategy, check this out: The Social Triangle™ was featured in a book by the OG Godfathers of Internet Marketing, Jay Abraham and Rich Schefren! So, if you don't believe me, BELIEVE THEM. LOL.

And if you want to see more examples so you can create posts of your own, be sure to grab my top 100 Organic Social Media posts! You'll see loads of great examples that we are updating regularly!

After creating a video that reached 1,000,000 people organically, Molly developed her "Go Live And Monetize" method, helping businesses to get clients with video. By staying ahead of trends like AI and chatbots, she stays on the cutting edge of what is coming next so her clients can make the most out of this rapidly changing space.

Combining her social media expertise, and twenty years of performance experience on stages from New York to Las Vegas, her most recent viral video hit a reach of 39 million! Molly has been featured by Be.live, ManyChat, Social Media Marketing World, Traffic & Conversion Summit, *Inc magazine*, *Forbes*, *Entrepreneur* and more.

Her book *Finding My Awesome* allows kiddos of all ages to celebrate their unique sense of awesome and live a life of confidence & joy.

Download my top 100 Social Media Engagement posts that have led to millions of video views, opt-ins, and sales.

TOP 100 SOCIAL MEDIA ENGAGEMENT POSTS

PLUS, an organic social mini course to make sure you have the strategy behind these posts so you can take them and make them your own!

Top 100 Organic Social Media Posts: https://molly.live/ep100

# A Website: Your 24/7 Sales Force

## MISSI HATFIELD

In "real life", also known as in-person conversation, you have seven seconds to make an initial impression. Seven seconds for someone to make every assumption about you, i.e., are you nice, are you an expert, are you fun to talk with, are you a resource? Studies show a website only has three seconds! Three seconds is the average attention span for viewers to decide if your website is going to offer what they are looking for! That isn't much, so you need to make every second count.

### FIRST: WHY HAVE A WEBSITE?

1. You want an online presence – A website gives you that presence and allows you to reach a wider audience. You can use your website to share information about your products and services, as well as communicate with potential customers.

2. Generating leads and sales – A website can help you generate leads and sales. You can use your website to showcase your products or services and provide potential customers with easy access to them. You can also use it to capture leads and build relationships with potential customers.

3. Building credibility and trust – A website can help you build credibility and trust with potential customers. You can use your website to provide information about your business, your products, and your services. This helps to build trust with potential customers who are more likely to make a purchase.

4. Connecting with customers – A website can also help you connect with customers and build relationships. You can use your website to share news, updates, and provide support. This helps to build loyalty and trust with customers.

5. Cost-effective marketing – A website is a cost-effective way to market your business. You can use your website to reach a wider audience, provide information about your business, and generate leads and sales.

In your precious three seconds, make sure the most important information on your website is prominently displayed and easy to understand.

### SECOND: DESIGN
The overall design and layout of your website should be clean and simple, with easy-to-read text and a logical navigation structure. Avoid clutter and distracting elements that make it harder for a visitor to focus on the key information you are offering.

### THIRD: CONTENT
1. Homepage – Your homepage provides the first impression and a chance to clearly explain who you are, what you offer, and what visitors can expect to find. A call to action, such as signing up for a newsletter or making a purchase is a must.

2. Navigation – Your website's navigation should be easy to use and understand. Make it easy for visitors to quickly find information on your website.

3. Content – This should be well-written, engaging, and relevant to your visitors.

4. Visuals – Visuals are an important part of any website. They can improve the visitor experience and draw attention to important content.

5. Contact information – Providing contact information is important for building trust with visitors. Include your business email address, business phone number, and possibly your physical address.

6. Social media links – Providing links to your social media accounts helps to build trust and allows visitors to stay connected with your business.

7. Footer – Include copyright information and links to important pages. You can also put the contact information in the footer for ease of use.

### FOURTH: PAGE SPEED

Optimize your website for speed. A slow-loading website is a major issue. Remember, you only have three seconds, so don't waste them waiting for a site to load. Using tools like Page Speed or GTX to test your site's performance will identify areas in need of improvement.

But wait. There's more:

Before you can capture your visitor with your brilliant website in only three seconds, they must find your website.

### FIFTH: SEO

Search Engine Optimization (SEO) is how you improve the visibility of your website or a web page in a search engine. Think about when you Google something. In general, the higher a website scores in SEO, the higher it will appear on a search engine results page.

## KEY ELEMENTS OF SEO

1. KEYWORDS: Keywords are words and phrases entered into search engines when looking for information. Use relevant and specific keywords that match words and phrases commonly used to search for your product or service.

2. ON-PAGE OPTIMIZATION: You can control the optimization with headlines, meta descriptions, and content. Optimizing, or using best practices, these elements for search engines will improve the visibility of your website in the search engine results.

3. LINK BUILDING: Search engines use links to determine the relevance and authority of a website. By building high-quality, relevant links to your website, you can increase the website's visibility in search results.

4. TECHNICAL ORGANIZATION: This includes the overall structure of your website, the code that runs it, mobile optimization, and load time. All of these will affect SEO results.

5. ANALYTICS and TRACKING: Analyzing your website traffic, user behavior, and the results of your SEO efforts is essential for making informed decisions about your optimization strategy.

SEO is a long-term process, and the results will not come overnight. But by following best practices and making continuous improvements, you can increase your website visibility, drive more traffic to your site, and increase your success.

Missi Hatfield is the co-owner of WebShotOne, a WordPress web development company specializing in "Building Websites that Build Businesses." An expert on the importance of having a website, what a website should look like, and protecting your website for your business. She is a 20-year veteran of the US Air Force, graduate of Barry University, former drill sergeant, author, and entrepreneur.

Missi is also a graduate of the National Speakers Association Speakers Academy where she received the peer-selected Spirit Award.

www.WebShotOne.com

Free Gift: Audit of your current website: https://webshotone.com/index.php/free-website-audit

*"The greatest thing in this world is not so much where we stand as in what direction we are moving."*
JOHANN WOLFGANG VON GOETHE

# Get Found: Be Your Own Sales Magnet

### KENDRA LEE

When you start your business, the first thing you need is customers. Their revenue gives you the fuel to not only survive, but to grow. The big question is, where do you find them?

Most business owners have never sold before and the thought of it feels intimidating. You are passionate about your services and they're valuable. You know why you're starting a business but aren't sure how you'll get the word out to get customers.

Those feelings of uncertainty, and sometimes fear, get in the way of your success. But they don't have to. There are five steps to build a sales plan and attract new customers.

## 1. GET YOUR GRABBER

I love the word grabber. When I think about grabbing prospects' attention, I picture reaching out and hooking them in. All their attention is focused on me because they're intrigued. They want to talk with me.

That's what you want to do with your target market. You want to have a grabber that draws them into conversation with you.

To get your grabber, list the problems your product or services solve for your target customer. Consider:

- What's top of mind that they are talking about right now?

- What's worrying them?

- What's hindering their productivity?

- Where could they increase revenue or reduce costs?

- Where is their customer satisfaction negatively impacted?

Once you have the list of problems, ask yourself:

- What's the biggest problem you can solve for them?

- Why is it a problem they can't solve without you?

- When does the problem happen?

- Where does the problem occur?

- Who in your target customers' world is impacted by the problem?

- How does your solution make things better for them if that problem no longer exists?

Pull it all together to create your grabber. Here's the formula:

Problem They Feel + Impact From The Problem + Results When It's Solved

Your grabber is the basis of all your lead generation and sales.

## 2. MAXIMIZE YOUR NETWORK FOR REFERRALS

As a new entrepreneur, finding your first few customers feels the most difficult. You have this great offering, but you don't have any proof. No existing customers to write Google testimonials or talk you up on social. Potentially no website or brochures.

While it's tempting to believe you need those things before you approach anyone to buy, stomp down that feeling. When I started KLA Group, I didn't have a website or brochure. I had career references, but no client references. That didn't stop me, and it shouldn't stop you. It takes bold confidence to pursue your first customers, but you already have that. You wouldn't be an entrepreneur if you didn't.

Still, let's not make the first sale harder than necessary. Begin with who you know. These are the people you'll be most comfortable with, so there is less risk of embarrassment if you aren't quite confident with your grabber yet.

- Open your phone, email, and social channels contact lists.

- Identify the people who could refer you to someone they know who might need your services.

- Plan to call each one. Use your grabber to articulate the value you offer. Tell them about your services. Ask who they know that you should speak with.

Even after you've been in business a long time, your network is still your best source of leads. These people know you, the value of your offerings, and will happily refer you if you just ask. Ask.

## 3. TURN YOUR WEBSITE INTO A LEAD MAGNET

Your website is your prospects' window into your world. It not only highlights your offerings, but also provides insight into you and your company, making you relatable.

Your website should also be a lead magnet, pulling your target audience to you.

- Optimize your website for searchers to find you by using keywords in your content. The best keywords are the words and phrases your target prospects use to find answers to the problems they have that you solve and to learn about the services you offer.

- Follow search engine optimization (SEO) best practices. Optimize your website with the correct meta tags, meta descriptions, and structure. Continually monitor it to ensure your site is healthy without errors and warnings. This is one area you will probably want outside assistance with.

- Include links to your website in all your social profiles. Use links when they fit your posts.

Once prospects reach your website, give them things they can engage with:

- Add resources your target visitors will find useful, such as blogs, guides, quizzes, and tutorials.

- If you have a newsletter, include a sign-up form.

- Gate your most valuable resources with a form to capture contacts' information.

- Post information about any events you'll be participating in with registration links. Encourage prospects to attend.

- Add videos that explain how you work with customers. Add informational videos answering commonly asked questions and things your top prospects should know.

SEO pulls prospects to your website. Valuable information and resources engage them and entice them to sign up. Now you have new people you've never met to whom you can reach out.

## 4. LOVE YOUR LIST

As you focus on marketing, your list grows with website downloads, referrals, social followers, event participants, and more. Not everyone will be ready to engage right away. For those people, you want a nurture strategy that keeps you visible with them until they are ready for your services.

One of the easiest nurture strategies is email. You have contacts' email addresses. They engaged with you and showed an interest. They like what you do. They are interested in what you share. They want to hear from you even though they aren't ready.

Stay in the forefront of their minds by showing your list some love. Five ideas to consider are:

- A newsletter

- Emailing links to new blogs as you post them

- Periodic email campaigns about new services, or reminders about your current offerings

- Invitations to events you're participating in

- Updates as your business grows and evolves

Another nurture strategy is social media. Posting frequently keeps you visible with your followers. The only drawback is that not all the prospects on your list may be followers.

Combine email and social media to create a powerful nurture strategy.

You work hard to build a list of prospects and only a small percentage may buy immediately. Plan to nurture the others. Don't let your hard work go to waste.

## 5. PUT YOUR METRICS TO WORK

As you can tell by now, you use many different strategies to get noticed and nurture prospects until they buy. You want to know what's working and what's not. That means measuring what you're doing.

Some metrics to monitor are:

- Sales

- Leads

- Referrals received

- New appointments set

- Website traffic, website health, and the number of forms filled

- Email opens, clicks, and replies

- Social growth

As you monitor your metrics, use them to draw insights and determine where to adjust. Know that marketing and sales take time. Make small adjustments before scrapping an approach entirely. Start by examining:

- Your grabber

- The target prospect and market

- How you are implementing the strategy

Often small tweaks can shift results in your favor.

## BUILD YOUR CUSTOMER ACQUISITION PLAN

Every entrepreneur without a sales background thinks they need to invest in expensive systems or hire others to help them find customers. That's simply not the case. Use the five steps to build your customer acquisition plan to attract new customers.

While you may need help writing content, developing email campaigns, creating your website, managing your SEO, or learning to sell, you are in control. Now you have a plan to confidently find new customers.

Kendra Lee is president and founder of KLA Group, an author, speaker, and new business development authority. Despite starting her sales career in accounting, failing IBM's entry level sales exam, and being told she couldn't sell without an engineering background, she entered sales and proved those nay-sayers wrong catapulting to the top 1% of salespeople in each company where she sold. She turned her knowledge of numbers into a lead generation approach that has propelled her clients' growth. Kendra founded KLA Group, a sales and marketing agency, to consult, train and "Do it For You." KLA Group helps SMB companies get more customers and increase revenue by using targeted lead generation and sales strategies that speak directly to your ideal prospects and highlight your company's uniqueness. Kendra is author of the books, *The Sales Magnet* and *Selling Against the Goal*.

## How to Ask For and Get Referrals the Easy Way

Use these five resources to propel you forward:

1. How to Ask For and Get Referrals the Easy Way. Use this nine-page free guide to take the reticence out of asking for referrals. I give you three ways and the best time to ask. It couldn't be easier!

2. 55 Marketing Activities to Reach Leads. Here are fifty-five different lead generation techniques to share your expertise, embrace video, expand with social media, and more. Mix and match to reach your target market and fill your sales funnel.

3. 12 Steps to Create Marketing Messages. Use this worksheet to write impactful messages that break through the noise and get noticed by your target market. Your prospects deserve to know how you can help them solve their problems.

4. Prospecting is Like a Cocktail Party. Watch this 2-minute video and discover how to change your perspective of prospecting and have fun with it. Remember, you're an expert. Nobody will represent your services like you will.

5. Call Guide for Prospecting & Sales Meetings. Use this free guide to plan referral conversations, sales meetings, and prospecting calls. You'll know exactly what you want to say to start the conversation, what to ask, and how to wrap up.

Use this nine-page guide to take the reticence out of asking for referrals. You get three easy phrases to ask and discover the best times to do it. Referrals are the fastest and easiest way to get new customers. Value: $67. Yours free: https://www.klagroup.com/How-to-Ask-For-Referrals

# How Affiliate Marketing Will Make You A Hero To Your Customers

JEN PERDEW

When you make a recommendation about a product or service to another person, and you are compensated for that referral, that's affiliate marketing. By making the introduction, you're the middleman.

You can't offer every solution to every businessperson's problem.

This is why you want to find trusted programs and partners to help bridge the gap between what your customers want or need and your products.

Affiliate marketing has been a huge part of our revenue at NAMS for the past fifteen years. About forty percent of our annual revenue comes from affiliate marketing. In fact, I just hit the 900K mark on one platform alone.

So pay attention to how powerful this selling and marketing strategy can be.

There are multiple ways to do affiliate marketing, but I will focus on the two that generate the most revenue for me.

## #1 CREATE CONTENT AND RECOMMENDATIONS AROUND A PRODUCT YOU ALREADY USE REGULARLY

It's so much easier for you when you do this. Why? Because it's authentic. Your customers see this, and you're more confident because you actually know the product well.

**Here's an example of one of my best affiliate campaigns:**

1. I created a digital downloadable product with ten templates to build simple product funnels.

2. When I delivered the product, I included a PDF of the templates, a video on how to use the templates, and a PDF overview of how to create sales funnels.

3. I also told folks about the tool I used to build those funnels. First, I gave them an affiliate link to click to start a free trial, then I told anyone who signed up for the trial to email me, and if they did, I would give them a share link to import the templates into their own app.

4. The product owner then sold people into the paid version of the product.

It was a win/win/win.

A win for me, a win for the affiliate vendor, and a win for the customer. I made their lives easier by recommending a tool I used *and* gave them a way to shortcut their workload by giving them an importable link to my own funnel.

## WHAT IF YOU DON'T NEED THE PRODUCT, BUT YOUR CUSTOMERS DO?

I *highly* recommend that you BUY the product, learn it, and use it.

For example, I teach people how to build their online businesses. Everyone needs an autoresponder system.

I use KEAP. But most of my clients don't need a platform like this one. They need something less expensive and complex that still has the ability to scale.

So, I pay for another system as a backup. I use the system in trainings, I know the system, and I recommend the system because it makes sense for my customers even though it's not a core piece of my business.

But I make enough money in commissions every month that it covers the cost for this system ten times over.

## YOU'LL OFTEN GET A PRODUCT REVIEW COPY FROM THE VENDOR.

Once I've looked at the review copy, and I've decided I want to promote the product, I go buy it. I buy all the products in the funnel that I believe my list can use.

The reason?

I want to see what the customer experiences.

I want to make sure the review product is the same as the product being sold.

I also want to know about the other products in the funnel so I can recommend those products. It really helps my conversions, and my affiliates *love* that, as do the customers. I tell my buyers, "Yes, you need this", or "No, don't buy this", etc. They buy what I offer because I'm so honest about whether or not the upsells are something they should get.

Operating with this kind of transparency increases my conversion rates and earnings per sale, which is a massive win for me and the vendors whose products I pitch.

Anything that helps your customers use and implement the product successfully works!

My challenge to you is to find a way you can embed affiliate offers in your own products.

Here's a quick and easy tip: Put a resource guide in all of your products and on your website that points people to your favorite tools. It works like a charm. All without sending an email.

## #2 SENDING EMAILS TO PRODUCTS
Regardless of what you read online, email marketing is not dead.

Email has the highest return on investment of any other marketing strategy out there—by about tenfold.

Ninety percent of my revenue comes from email marketing. It's not all sales emails, but every email has some call to action, which is then monetized.

For example, read a blog post, watch this free training . . . you get the picture.

But I do sell a lot of affiliate products through email.

Your email style is something you're going to have to create and massage, so test it and work on a structure and style that works for both you and your readers.

I've tried multiple types of emails. There's only one style that works for me: story emails with detailed information about the offer. I've tried short-and-sweet emails without a story. When I do, my members revolt. They want the story.

In my ten years of doing this, I've only had about fifteen people tell me they wished my emails were shorter.

But let's talk more in depth regarding marketing affiliate products with email.

I'm successful at this because I'm methodical about how I go about it.

In fact, just recently, I went on vacation and ran multiple email campaigns to my list while I was gone. These were about 50% affiliate marketing and about 50% of my own product promotions.

I netted almost $12,000 in cash . . . all while away from the business.

These are the three things I always do in my promotional emails.

1.  I write my own emails. Affiliates will typically provide you with swipe files. These are emails they've written to make promoting easier for you. But so many other people use those swipe files word for word. If you're on multiple marketers' lists, you'll get the *exact* email copy in your inbox.

    I may use the swipe copy to get a feel for what I want to say, or an angle for my copy, but I write my own and create an email series that builds one upon another. For example, I may say "Yesterday I told you about (a specific feature), now let me tell you how to combine (feature 1) with (feature 2) to get more bang for your buck.

    This strategy helps increase my conversion rates and it also shows my reader that I *know* the product. It's more than just a generic email for a generic product I've never even used. And I'm helping to set my reader up for success.

2. I test the product to tell the reader how to implement or use the product. For example, there's a product I love and use frequently. When that vendor announced they were doing a big launch, I knew I wanted to be involved.

   While going through and implementing the product on my own site, I realized the product creator missed a *huge* selling point—and I remembered that issue.

   I thought that specific selling point was more beneficial to my members than the other features the vendor was listing.

   Because of this, I specifically created my email promotions around that one feature and how to benefit from it.

3. I always tell my readers about the other products in the funnel. I also buy them to see how useful they are for my members.

In all transparency, I've gotten many irritated emails about strategy #3 from people learning about affiliate marketing.

Why?

They don't want to buy the product to test it.

Listen, that's part of doing business. The only way you can pull off this strategy and make sure your customers are getting the best possible product and experience is to experience the whole funnel yourself.

As I said earlier, paying for my back-up autoresponder each month costs about $29. Just knowing how to use this autoresponder means that I typically get between $300-$400 per month in recurring commissions from that product.

I'll take those kinds of numbers any day of the week.

**The last big tip I want to give you on doing affiliate promotions with email:**

Stick with the promotion.

Some products and launches aren't going to resonate with your list. But make sure you put some real effort into the promotion.

*Rarely* will you ever see me send aa single email about an affiliate product.

We commit to a promotion, schedule it, create the content, and make tweaks along the way to increase our conversions. We find the angle that resonates with our members, and we tweak it more. When you stick with it, you'll do well, and your members will trust you to make high-quality recommendations.

When you buy the products to test a funnel and get set up for an affiliate promotion, send the receipts to your accountant. (That's called the Cost of Goods Sold!)

**Now I want you to look at the products your members will benefit from knowing about and start outlining your affiliate email promotion.**

It doesn't have to be a launch. Launches are great because there's built-in scarcity for your reader to take immediate action,

You can add scarcity of your own in your campaigns to run evergreen affiliate promotions a couple of times a year by adding your own scarcity. That might be a bonus, or a live training, or a Facebook Group where questions can be answered but the bonus goes away after a certain amount of time.

I hope you've seen ways affiliate marketing can help your customers, build a high level of trust and rapport between you and them, and add additional income streams in your business.

The Novice to Advanced Marketing System (NAMS) was founded by David Perdew over fifteen years ago. David recently retired and his daughter, Jen Perdew, who has been working at NAMS since 2011,purchased the business. The Novice to Advanced Marketing System is a step-by-step system focusing on Team, Training, and Tools to help novice to advanced businesspeople build a simple, scalable, and sustainable business.

Jen is now the President and CEO of NAMS and comes from a customer service, operations, and employee training background.

Jen has always loved digging in and getting her hands dirty with automation and coaching. Jen's an implementor and focuses on moving her clients as quickly as possible down the path to success. NAMS is one of the most successful online communities today, specializing in training and proprietary productivity software tools.

If you'd like to learn more about how to either get started with affiliate marketing or how to implement more advanced strategies, click the link and grab my top-selling affiliate checklists for free! (Regularly $47) https://nams.ws/EAPLS

*"Live as if you were to die tomorrow.*
*Learn as if you were to live forever."*
MAHATMA GANDHI

# How to Use Webinars to Grow Your Business

LAURA BRIGGS

**W**ebinars, or online training opportunities, are wonderful for sharing valuable insights with your audience over a focused training period. When you are trying to decide whether to offer webinars, consider your comfort level on camera, your technical savvy, and the time commitment required to create a winning webinar.

## WHAT ARE WEBINARS?

Webinars are video based trainings that provide information, education, or entertainment to an audience. Typically, webinars are free and are designed to help people better understand a process, think through common mistakes, or take some initial action steps in solving a bigger problem.

Most webinars in the business world are forty-five to ninety minutes long. Longer webinars, such as ninety-minute webinars, are typically recommended for people who have extensive experience in running webinars, as it can take a great deal of work and attention to keep people focused for that much time. When used properly, webinars can help bring in new clients to your company and allow you to create content that can be repurposed.

## WHAT CAN WEBINARS REALLY DO FOR YOUR BUSINESS?

It takes a substantial amount of work and even some investments in software in order to be successful using webinars. This is why they are more of an advanced marketing tool.

Webinars have some incredible payoffs that can help move people further down along the marketing funnel when you know how to use them.

For example, someone who interacts with a Facebook ad, a social media post, or an email newsletter from you may not have enough trust and knowledge in your ability to understand their problem or believe you have the solution to their problem. However, over the course of a webinar, you get to share your personal story, address common questions, and lay out a process or teaching series that helps people feel more confident in you and your knowledge about their problem.

In many cases, the webinar handles a small portion of the person's issue and then they are introduced to your potential solution, whether that be a coaching session, purchasing a digital product, buying a book, or something else. Webinars can bring in new leads, introduce people to your expertise and thought leadership, deliver great value, and set people up to buy.

Free webinars are positioned as a value-ad for your attendees because you will be giving them valuable and helpful information over the course of the webinar. At the end of the webinar, you may use this opportunity to present something to them for sale, although you are not required to do so. Some people offer a series of free webinars simply as an opportunity to get their name out there. Webinars can also form valuable repurposing material for your content marketing. For example, a forty-five-minute webinar could be turned into multiple blog posts or an email series, smaller videos for YouTube, and so much more. Here's a quick example of how a forty-five-minute webinar might flow:

- *5-7 minutes: introduction, welcome, explain agenda*

- *1-2 minutes: explain the problem the watcher is facing*

- *20-22 minutes: share content, interact with audience*

- *10 minutes: present offer, hold Q & A for watchers*

Webinars are great opportunities to connect with your potential audience in real time and to answer their questions, showing that you're a real person who deeply understands their needs.

## WHAT ARE THE CHALLENGES WITH WEBINARS?

Although webinars hold a tremendous amount of potential for growing your business, they are not necessarily easy to pull off. It can take a lot of work to create your outline for your content material, to practice running your webinar, to set up the back-end technology for anything you'll sell, to drive traffic to the webinar, and to continue to follow up with people after the fact.

Many webinars require a great deal of practice in advance, and public speaking can be challenging for people. It's a good idea to test any of your webinar software and your entire slideshow well in advance to make sure everything works correctly. Don't aim for a perfect webinar your first time out of the gate. Instead, it's far better to focus on delivering a good experience for people who are in attendance.

My very first webinar had only two people on the call. The webinar software hid how many people were in attendance, so they had no idea if there were 100 people on the call and both of the people ended up buying a $1,000 offer at the conclusion of the webinar. While part of that felt distressing because only two people attended, it did lead to a 100% conversion rate.

The primary goal is for you to get some experience during your first couple of webinars. You'll learn some lessons and go from there to improve the experience for everyone in attendance. You do not necessarily need to teach a new topic every time you create a new webinar. In fact, you can find one or two topics that you use over and over again when creating your webinar strategy.

## WHAT TOOLS DO YOU NEED FOR WEBINARS?
A couple of core pieces of technology are essential for success with webinars. These are a microphone, a good camera, a slideshow technology such as Canva, Keynote, or PowerPoint, and a tool to facilitate the webinar itself, such as Zoom, Go To Webinar, or YouTube Live. You will also likely need a place where people can register to attend the webinar, which can be handled by some features in other tools mentioned here, such as Zoom. Zoom allows you to set up free registration. If you use other tools, such as LeadPages or your email service provider's landing pages, you will also need to make sure an email automation is set up to send people reminders about the event and to send them a recording of the replay.

## BEST PRACTICES FOR WEBINARS
One of the most important things you can do in any webinar is to plan for success by making sure that if anything bad happens—such as your technology doesn't function properly, only a handful of people show up, or you're nervous—that the people in attendance still have a good experience. This

primarily comes down to your chosen topic and style of presentation.

## FOCUS ON ONE KEY PROBLEM OR PROCESS

Most people try to cram way too much information into a webinar. For example, you might not want to attend a webinar that's called Fifteen Steps Towards Finally Losing That Last Fifty Pounds. That feels overwhelming for attendees and requires a great deal of preparation from you. You'd be far better off thinking about the first three steps someone needs to take and presenting that over a forty-five to sixty-minute webinar.

## DELIVER A CLEAR PREMISE IN THE TITLE

Your title should tell people exactly what they're going to achieve by attending the webinar. It could be:

- Complete your entire meal plan for the next month, or

- Learn how to market your freelance business in two hours a week or less.

These are great examples of clear premises that someone will feel is well worth their time. Remember, your attendees are setting aside valuable time to attend a webinar, and if they're not familiar with you and your business offering just yet, you want to load them up with value and show how much you know about your field.

## PRACTICE IN ADVANCE

Explore all of your technology well in advance, including recording capability. Run a test webinar to see how things look and sound, and make sure you try out any additional features you intend to use during the actual webinars, such as live polls.

## TELL PEOPLE WHAT TO EXPECT AT THE OUTSET OF THE WEBINAR

There's nothing better than setting up someone's expectations by telling them exactly what you're going to dive into. This should include things like a short five minute or less introduction about you, then a dive into the topic, then time for questions and a possible presentation of your offer. Some people conclude with their offer and then allow questions so the offer remains up on the webinar screen.

## DON'T EXPECT TREMENDOUS RESULTS YOUR FIRST FEW WEBINARS

It is certainly possible to achieve outstanding results with webinars the first couple of times you offer them, but don't hold yourself to a high standard such as trying to get 100 people to attend the first one or expecting everyone to buy. You may not even sell anything during your first webinar, which is one of those reasons I mentioned above. Have I mentioned that I love those tools that don't tell your attendees how many people are in the room?

Laura Briggs is a freelance writer and digital marketing strategist. With over ten years of experience, she has worked with over 400 clients all over the world. She's a three-time TEDx speaker and the author of five books: *How to Start Your Own Freelance Writing Business, The Six Figure Freelancer, How to Become a Virtual Assistant, Remote Work for Military Spouse,* and *Content is King.*

Plan Your Money-Making Automated Webinar in a Weekend

LAURA BRIGGS
THE FREELANCE COACH

Get access to this free 37-page planner to help you title, outline, and get ready to produce your first money-making webinar in just one weekend.

Link to free gift: https://authorlaurabriggs.ck.page/3c7a287919

*"Writing a book gives you the opportunity to gift the world with pleasure or knowledge—if you write well, it can do both."*
LINDA STIRLING

# Books To Build Authority & Attract Clients

LINDA STIRLING

I think it goes without saying that a book will benefit you in your business. There are a number of reasons why people don't write one, however.

Perhaps you believe:

- You don't know how to get started.

- You believe it will take too much time.

- You're afraid you don't have enough to say.

- You believe there are already too many books on your topic.

- You believe people will judge you, so that stops you from moving forward.

There may be other reasons you are telling yourself you can't write a book.

I'm going to show you why those reasons or any other reasons that you may come up with are not valid. Along the way, I will show you how to get visibility for your book, which in turn will help bring visibility to your business.

## YOU DON'T KNOW HOW TO GET STARTED

Here are a couple of ways that can make the process easier.

1. Go through your existing blogs or other written material. Consider how these might be organized to form the framework of your book.

2. Get into the habit of jotting down ideas. Collect those, and over time they will form the skeleton of your chapters.

3. Look at books similar to the one you want to write. Examine each book's table of contents to spark ideas for your own book. Next, look at the reviews for those books. Are there comments about information that was left out or information that wasn't clear? What other comments are made about the book that would be helpful in creating your own book?

Adopt one of these methods and then schedule time to write, whether it's once a day, on the weekend, or perhaps during an extended weekend devoted exclusively to writing.

## YOU BELIEVE IT WILL TAKE TOO MUCH TIME

Books can be long, but that doesn't mean they have to be. Some of the shortest books get the best reviews. These days, people don't have time to wade through page after page in order to get to the meat of what they want to learn. For this reason, short books are more popular than ever.

Do you know that Amazon has several categories devoted solely to short books?

eBooks can be as short as a single page! I suspect you have more to say than what can be said in a single page. Fortunately, books that are at least twenty pages can be printed. I recommend that you write forty pages or more because that gives you an actual spine on your book. This creates a book that also has a more pleasing appearance when you gift someone your book or have it available at conferences and other events.

If the nature of what you're sharing lends itself to diagrams or some other kind of image, those can quickly expand your page count.

Many people can write forty pages in one or two sittings. You can too when you start with a framework. Keep in mind forty book pages are not the same as forty pages in a standard document. Depending on the size of the book that you choose, a forty-page book might be as little as twenty-five typed pages. If you add images, that further decreases the number of words you need to write.

Even if it takes you a month, having a book will make you more credible to the people you do business with. It can also open doors for speaking engagements, give you credibility as a coach, and more.

## YOU'RE AFRAID YOU DON'T HAVE ENOUGH TO SAY

You'd be surprised how quickly a book can be written once you take the step of fleshing out a few chapters. Drawing on one's experiences and crafting a book with an engaging storytelling approach is a style that readers love, so don't be afraid to populate your book with storytelling. Sharing your story is also a way for readers to feel connected to you.

Consider asking people you already work with what kind of information that you already share that they find most valuable. This may spark ideas you hadn't considered.

Keep in mind that people prefer information that is *short and actionable.*

## YOU BELIEVE THERE ARE TOO MANY BOOKS ON THE SUBJECT ALREADY

Actually, you *want* the marketplace to already contain books similar to the book you're planning to write. If there aren't any books like yours, this means there isn't a demand for them. The presence of at least several books on the subject you're writing about will mean that when people look for your topic, your book has a good chance of coming up.

As shared before, look at similar books and determine how you can make your book answer questions others left unanswered or didn't expand enough on. Sometimes the reviews will say that the author rambled. That's a perfect reason for you to keep your writing short.

It's important to know that people resonate with different writing styles. Your style might appeal perfectly to them.

## YOU'RE AFRAID PEOPLE WILL JUDGE YOU

There will always be someone who will! That's just part of allowing yourself to be visible in the marketplace. Chances are, the people judging you haven't written a book themselves. Don't allow naysayers or your own fear to keep you from writing a book that could escalate your visibility and potentially build a solid group of followers, perhaps even fans.

## SETTING YOUR BOOK UP FOR SUCCESS

There are some core elements needed to make your book appear professional.

- You want a cover that fits in with similar books. Readers buy books that feel like they will resonate.

That means when they look at your book, they want to have the feeling "this looks similar to books that I like."

- Your book should be edited well. A lack of professional editing sends the message that you are sloppy—not a message you want to send to people with whom you want to do business.

- Set your book up in the correct categories. You may find these by looking at the categories listed for other books like yours. A tool I use to get proper categories is Publisher Rocket. You can find it here: https://thepublishingcircle.com/rocket.

- When listing your book, you'll be asked to list keywords. These should be words that are logical choices for people who would be looking for a book like yours. In addition to single words that are used as keywords, you can include keyword phrases. An example of a keyword phrase might be *Exercise for women over 50.*

- The blurb you write for your book should be something you put a lot of thought into. This is your sales message and if that message doesn't resonate with potential buyers, they will move on to the next book. If you're not skilled at writing blurbs, there are people who will do this for you. You can find people who will write blurbs at Fiverr.com or Upwork.com.

- As soon as you launch your book, you need to quickly acquire at least fifteen reviews. Amazon has shared that they give more algorithm juice to books with fifteen or more reviews. This is especially important during the week you release your book. These reviewers should be people who typically read books like yours. This is important because it gives information to set up the algorithm so your book will fall into the right categories when people are searching. For example, if your book is about building confidence but the readers who leave reviews are people who typically only purchase books in the romance genre, that doesn't give the algorithm the right kind of information to make your book show up when people search for it. Amazon's policy is to only allow people to leave reviews who have had an Amazon account for at least six months and have purchased within that time frame. You'll want to ask your potential reviewers about this before they try to leave a review. You'll also need to be patient because reviews don't necessarily show up right away.

## WRITING A BOOK ISN'T ENOUGH

You have to market your book so it will remain visible to potential buyers. Here are a few ways to keep your book in front of readers.

- The easiest way is to run ads. At minimum, you'll want to become familiar with the Amazon advertising program. You don't need to limit yourself to Amazon, however. Placing an ad at a place such as Fussy Librarian or Book Gorilla might get you more attention for your book. You'll need to experiment to find the best spots to advertise.

- Write articles and share portions of your book in them. Places such as Medium.com will allow you to put a link to your book at the end of the article.

- Look for podcasts where you can share some of the lessons or insights from your book. By the way, the fact that you've written a book isn't news. You should always look for an angle that will benefit the listeners of the podcast. Highly successful authors often book several podcasts a day when their book is first released. This can propel them to the top of the charts. You may not want to have that kind of frequency, but at least getting on podcasts once in a while will help you maintain the visibility of your book.

- There are many other ways of marketing but employing at least the methods listed here will help your book maintain its presence in the marketplace.

Think of the people you want to serve with your book. Imagine them holding your book in their hands, reading and benefiting from what you've shared.

Visualize yourself opening a box that contains your book. That's going to be a proud moment.

Hold on to visions like these as you write!

An international bestselling author herself, Linda has worked in publishing for decades and is the author of 56 books in various genres and under multiple pseudonyms. She often speaks and teaches at events around the country. Her publishing house, The Publishing Circle, is described as "embracing a new paradigm in publishing." Because her company accepts limited works, she also teaches writers how they can either find a traditional publisher or self-publish. You can find out more about her publishing company at www.ThePublishingCircle.com.

Follow the guidance in this planner and you'll be ahead of the game when it comes time to write, publish, and launch your book. You can get it here:

https://thepublishingcircle.com/LaunchPlanner

*"Always do your best. What you plant now, you will harvest later."*
OG MANDINO

# Be A Superstar Salesperson: The Non-Salesy Approach

DANNY CREED

I 've been an entrepreneur and a salesperson most of my life. I've also had the privilege of training some very successful entrepreneurs worldwide. The main question I am asked is always about the essential skills they need to learn to thrive as an entrepreneur.

My answer: LEARN TO SELL

Selling is a skill. It is a skill that anyone can learn. And to be a successful woman in business today, you must be skillful at sales. But don't tell me you are not a salesperson. We are all salespeople in some form. If you've ever asked for a raise, you're in sales. If you've ever negotiated with children, you're in sales. But, if you want to be in business, it is imperative that you can sell your idea to bankers, investors, partners, and employees. In addition, you must sell your vision for the future to your family, friends, and spouses to earn support for your dreams.

You must know how to sell. However, the process of selling has drastically changed. The people who understand this shift in what the public will tolerate are winning at sales. The old approach to selling is unacceptable, although many sales trainers are still teaching this ancient approach. It's the approach that gives us the fear and loathing of most salespeople. The image of the fast-talking pitch person who tells more than listens quickly disappears and is replaced by sales professionals who ask more than tell. They are world-class listeners and problem solvers whose goal is to become a trusted advisor to their customers.

Power selling by simply perfecting the art of having a great conversation is particularly enticing for women in business. Through this approach, you throw out the window all preconceived ideas on the sales process. There's no big pitch moment or sneaky hard-sell tactics here. Instead, it's non-salsey. This approach is comfortable, simple, engaging, and effective. Selling by having a great conversation sounds easy but requires significant skills and a tremendous amount of strategy.

Here are my eight steps to build your conversational sales process for selling anything, at any price.

1. ELIMINATE THE FEAR OF BEING SOLD: If you're going to sell a prospect or a customer, let them know upfront why you're there. Most of the time, they understand why you're there. They know it's your goal to sell them your product, service, or idea. The key is what you tell them about why you're there. If you come to the meeting and begin to TELL them why they should buy your product, your prospect will immediately close you out and move into a defensive attitude. And, just as they thought, you will try to force something

on them. Our conversational approach begins with a specific strategy of turning those tables. My goal is always to eliminate their fear of being sold as quickly as possible. The best way to do that is to simply suggest something like this: *"I have a great product/service/ idea; in fact, it's had spectacular results with people like you. However, it is just not right for everyone. So, would it be okay for me to ask you four or five questions to discover together if it might be right for you? And, if it is, we'll do some business; if we learn it isn't, I've made a great new connection."*

2. STOP TELLING: No one likes to be told anything, so stop believing that selling is about telling. It's not. Grocery list selling has gone the way of the dodo bird. When you get in front of a prime prospect, the last thing they want is for a salesperson to *tell* them all the reasons they should buy and then ask them to pick the ones that interest them. A prospect could care less about all the benefits you offer. They only care about those few that might mean something to them, so stop talking and stop assuming and begin to ask questions.

3. Now, HAVE A CONVERSATION, ASK QUESTIONS, THEN LISTEN: Listening is the lost art of business today. If you become known as a great listener, customers will seek you out. That kind of success begins with asking questions. Your goal in asking questions is to understand the customer's/prospect's needs from the customer's/prospect's point of view. And their point of view is all that matters. So be strategic; ask questions to drive a productive conversation toward your product. Come up with four or five questions that are conversational but businesslike. I sometimes like to start with a positive-based question such as, *"One*

*of the perks of what I do is that I get to meet successful business people every day. What do you do every day to maintain a positive attitude?"* Be careful here. Never ask a prospect what problems they have or what keeps them up at night. Why? Because a strong-willed businesswoman or man will most definitely take offense to your insinuation that they have issues. In their mind, they have challenges and opportunities but not problems.

4.  NOW LISTEN, REALLY LISTEN: Here's where you perfect the art of listening for clarity. If you listen closely to what the prospect is saying, and they perceive that you are actively listening, something magical happens.

    Your prospect will TELL you how to sell them.

    They will tell you absolutely what their needs are from their point of view, and they will tell you what you need to do to sell them. They now want to work with you because you might be the first and only salesperson they have ever met who actually acts as if you care about them. So don't do anything other than listen.

5.  NOW, SHOW THEM YOU LISTENED: Say, *"What I heard you say was ___. Did I get that right?"* Restate each need your prospect/customer has revealed to you for clarity. Don't talk at length; just clarify that you understand everything they have told you. So, when you ask the right questions, you give your prospect/customer proof you were listening by restating what you heard. Now you've earned the right to use the three magic words in selling, "You told me . . ." Use this phrase to lock down what they told you, and now

you can discuss how your product/service or idea can solve your customer's needs.

6. CLOSE YOUR DEAL: Closing a sale never needs to be the big finale where all discussions lead. There's no need for cute closing lines or heavy-handed tactics. Closing a deal should be nothing more than the next logical step, and you want to keep this simple and natural. Your closing script should be something such as, *"When we started our conversation today, we agreed we would discover together if it made sense that we should work together. And based on what you just told me, I think it just makes sense that we should move forward. So, can we sign the agreement now?"*

Women in business and women who sell must be focused on showcasing positive attitudes. They must have a dogged determination and an unequaled work ethic. You must be a possibility thinker instead of exhibiting a survivor mentality. You have to put your whole heart into selling. Selling has often been called a transfer of enthusiasm. The more enthusiastic and convinced you are about what you are selling, the more contagious this enthusiasm will be and the more your customers will sense it and act on it. Consumers today—your prospects and customers—are emotional creatures. They are making their buying decisions based on emotions more than ever. This is why you must honestly care about their hopes, wishes, needs, and vision. Personal and professional development expert Brian Tracy told me once that caring was the essential, critical element in successful selling.

Your goal must be to walk, talk, and smile as a confident, top sales professional. However, you must position yourself as a consultant more than a salesperson. You must see yourself as a trusted advisor, a counselor, a visionary, and a problem solver more than anything else. Position yourself as someone who will listen and understand and offer real-world solutions.

If you want to be the best salesperson in your chosen field, dedicate yourself to continuous learning. If you're going to earn more in the future, you must always add skills and track trends. And today, you will be an A-list standout just by becoming overwhelmingly curious. Stop telling people what they need. Instead, ask them what they need. Ask many questions, act like you care about their answer, and listen closely. You will be amazed at what your prospects might tell you.

Master these things and quickly move into the top 1% of your chosen field. When you make conversational selling a habit, you'll soon learn that you will become a world-class saleswoman, helping people and potentially changing lives simply by having a great conversation.

Danny Creed is a professional and certified business and executive coach. He is a noted sales and leadership trainer, best-selling author, international keynote, and workshop speaker who is an acclaimed business turnaround expert.

Danny's personal coach and mentor is the legendary Brian Tracy. He is a certified business coach, executive coach, and sales trainer with over 15,000 logged coaching hours. In addition, he's an entrepreneur with 15 successful start-up businesses to his credit and over 400 business turnarounds. Coach Dan is the unprecedented seven-time recipient of the FocalPoint International Brian Tracy Award of Sales Excellence and CXO Outlooks "10 Most Inspiring Transformational Coaches, Globally – 2022."

Danny Creed is an internationally best-selling author of six business and motivational books, including the bestseller CHAMPIONS NEVER MAKE COLD CALLS and THRIVING in BUSINESS.

Dan is involved in community and volunteer work and, when time allows, a professional musician.

*"A customer is the most important visitor on our premises, he is not dependent on us. We are dependent on him. He is not an interruption in our work. He is the purpose of it. He is not an outsider in our business. He is part of it. We are not doing him a favor by serving him. He is doing us a favor by giving us an opportunity to do so."*
MAHATMA GANDHI

# Creating Attraction Magnets with Ease

NICOLE DEAN

How is it that some entrepreneurs, coaches, experts, authors seem to be visible everywhere? They always have something to say. Something to share. Something to offer.

Yet, when you look at their content, they sure don't look like they are slaving away over their computer every minute of every day. I mean, heck, your favorite Abundance Coach is posting from her RV, looking well-rested and relaxed. Your favorite Personal Development Expert is posting from her pool!

Either they have a closet full of content elves brainstorming and researching ideas for them, or they have a shortcut or a secret that they aren't sharing.

Meanwhile, you stare at a blank screen and wonder what the heck to say today!

I can reassure you they have a secret. I'll share it with you, along with a bunch of free shortcuts, too.

So what is the secret? Most of the coaches out there are using either templates or an even bigger helper.

## DONE-FOR-YOU OR BRANDABLE CONTENT

What is it exactly? Coaches and experts purchase content that is in "draft" mode or that's brandable. They use it like a template that is already partially filled in. They edit it and customize it as much or as little as they'd like. The end result is a unique piece of content they are able to share with their followers.

You can envision social media templates, for instance. You might find one with the text "What's your favorite podcast/ audio book to listen to when (insert activity)?" The content is already there and you just fill in the blank with something related to your audience.

You get to connect with your audience without having to think up ideas.

Just customize it and it turns into: What's your favorite podcast to listen to while cleaning the house? Cooking? Walking the dog? Driving?

Then replace the picture on it with a picture of you or a picture you took to make it more personal. Change the colors to match your brand. Once you've personalized your graphic, you post it along with a caption about your favorite podcast and why. It creates instant engagement in a truly authentic way.

For instance, if I used that template to connect with my audience, I might change it to: "What are your favorite audiobooks to listen to while getting some fresh air?"

I would replace the photo on the template with a photo I took of me with my airpods while on a hike this summer. I spent the summer camping in an RV (social proof of my adventurous lifestyle).

Then I just need a caption, right? I might go with something such as: "I've been traveling and am looking for some inspiration to listen to while getting fresh air this summer. I am not a fan of podcasts (I'll save that for another discussion) but I love audiobooks! I'm looking for anything related to personal development and am currently listening to Gabby Bernstein's 'You Are The Guru' and loving it. What personal development books have changed your life? I'm very interested in books written by women and would love a lot of diversity. I'm so excited to learn from you!"

Easy peasy. Do you see how a simple "cookie cutter" piece of content can become something that connects you to potential clients and customers? How it can set you up as the leader even if you don't have all the answers?

We've covered that done-for-you content is pretty powerful stuff. But what kind of content comes ready to personalize and profit?

You can get coaching forms, content kits, planners, emails, scripts, workbooks, social media posts, sales copy, and even entire coaching programs.

What are some types of attraction magnets that you can create, either with our help or on your own?

## PLANNERS AND WORKBOOKS

The planners we create at CoachGlue are robust and have exercises in each section. You could easily take a workbook, rebrand it to your colors, add an "About Me" section, along with a call-to-action such as "sign up for a discovery call" or "sign up for my free webinar here!" in the planner. Turn it into a pdf (which is super easy and free to do), then post a video on Instagram or a post on Facebook saying "Who wants my free social media planner? Just DM me and I'll send it to you!"

Imagine if you are a social media manager or a consultant and you have people coming to you who need help with their social media. You send them the planner and ask if they have any questions or if there's anything you can do for them. You send them the links to sign up for your free training or a discovery call. When you do that, the right people will hire you. Or maybe you send people to your tools page where you list your favorite social media tools—using your affiliate links, of course. This creates multiple streams of income. And it all starts with a workbook you didn't even have to create!

## CHALLENGES

You can also turn a workbook into a 5-day challenge and then offer that challenge on all of the places your audience hangs out.

Or, again, if you don't want to use the content we create, this is another way for you to create an attraction magnet on your own. Just map out the five steps a person would need to take to accomplish a goal.

Once you're clear on the five steps, you'll turn each step into a daily lesson. Include the exercises as printable activity sheets with each lesson.

Then offer the challenge with a set start date so you can build a community around it. People sign up for the challenge. You grow your lists.

It's the combination of your leadership, the activities/exercises, and community where the magic is created.

BUT ... this method again works best if you choose a topic that naturally leads into something else that you offer, such as a group coaching program, done-for-you service, or consulting.

So, what is the introduction to what you offer? If you are a money mindset coach, then start with "5-Day Uncovering & Healing Your Money Wounds." Help people start to expose and heal some of their money wounds, then offer your group coaching for greater transformation.

My wish for you is that your business is effortless and elegant. We all wake up with the capacity for decision making and creativity. Don't waste yours trying to create ALL the things from scratch. Use shortcuts when they make sense without apology. The goal is to make an income and make an impact. Don't second guess how you accomplish those things.

 Since 2005, Nicole Dean has been helping savvy and smart women entrepreneurs to stop the overwhelm, calm the comparison-itis, and show up, share, and shine and take steps to finally build active and passive wealth. Her clients are multi-six-figure successes who are burned out trying to do all the things. They don't need more knowledge or to sit through yet another video course: they need a smart and safe big sister who is on their side, ready to help them

build the lifestyle, business, and wealth of their dreams. The world is full of magic. Build a business that lets you explore and enjoy all of it.

Want a super easy to create social media graphics? Use Canva templates! Head to the link to get twenty free and completely customizable templates designed for coaches. You can use them over and over. https://coachglue.com/social-bonus/

*"The power of visibility can never
be underestimated."*
MARGARET CHO

# Creating Online Visibility
# On LinkedIn

## BRYNNE TILLMAN

Y ou have chosen entrepreneurship, most likely because you love what you do, you are really good at it,
and you are confident that people will pay you for it.
Congratulations, most people never get here.

But what you may not have realized, by choosing to be an
entrepreneur you have landed in a sales and marketing role.

*"If I just had more conversations with my ideal buyers, my
business would thrive,"* says almost every entrepreneur I've
ever talked to.

Chances are that if you had more inbound conversations,
people would fall in love with you and your solution, and you
wouldn't have to worry about prospecting.

However, the reality is that inbound opportunities rarely
happen on their own. There is a lot of outbound that we have
to do in order to get conversations with the right people at the
right time.

There are many ways to open up opportunities, including cold calling, email campaigns, networking, paid advertising, and social selling.

LinkedIn is the most powerful digital platform to attract, teach, and engage our targeted audience, yet most entrepreneurs on the platform say . . .

1. I have thousands of connections, but no conversations.

2. When I ask for conversations from prospects, I get ghosted.

3. I share content, yet no one engages.

4. Everyone says I need to use LinkedIn, but I can't figure out how to do it successfully.

Here's what's broken:

1. Profiles are self-centered vs. value-centric

2. Cold calling on LinkedIn

3. Connect and pitch

4. Connect and forget

5. Random acts of social engagement

6. Post and ghost

7. Sharing topics that sales wants to talk about, NOT what prospects want to consume

8. Not leveraging referrals and getting permission to name drop

There are thousands of LinkedIn trainers and coaches, each with their own perspective of what social selling means to them. I am not going to get on my high horse and tell you that my way is right and everyone else is wrong. You have to take the following tips and strategies that have been proven incredibly effective and make them your own. Use your own voice and be authentic.

The most important LinkedIn outreach mindset is to treat the person on the other side of the message the same way you would if they were on the other side of the table.

These are not leads, they are people. Imagine yourself at a trade show, conference, business card exchange, or networking event as you read through this chapter.

With that in mind, my definition is . . .

"Social Selling is about building rapport, providing real value, and developing trust and credibility by being a resource . . . understanding that the sales will come when the time is right."

My company has been leveraging LinkedIn for almost two decades and we have learned a ton about how to convert connections into meaningful conversations that lead to sales. Through my A/B testing of different approaches, styles, techniques, messaging templates, prospecting campaigns, content strategies, and beyond, I have developed a playbook designed to help entrepreneurs master LinkedIn for sales.

There is no easy button or magic wand. I have no pixie dust. What I do have is a daily routine that includes everything an entrepreneur needs to do to grow their business by leveraging the power of LinkedIn.

Before you begin prospecting, it is vital that you position your profile to be value centric; to be the landing page that attracts, teaches, and engages your buyers. All roads lead back to your profile. And, even if you aren't using LinkedIn, well, your buyers are. They are vetting vendors and LinkedIn is often the first place they go. Even if they Google you, LinkedIn will typically be in the first three results (go Google yourself and see what comes up).

The job of your profile is to convert your prospect from a lurker to an engager. To get them curious about how you can help them by teaching them something new that gets them thinking differently about their current situation. To get them to raise their hands and say, *"I'd like to learn more."*

The following is a checklist that will help you begin your social selling journey. While this is just the tip of the iceberg, if you embrace the following process, you will start more sales conversations on a consistent basis.

## ✓ BACKGROUND BANNER

We are all visual, so including a banner that represents your brand is important. Keep in mind that the perfect LinkedIn banner size has a 1:4 aspect ratio. If you don't have a marketing department to create a profile for you, there are a few options:

1. Canva is a free site where you can choose many options to create a perfect banner.

2. Fiverr.com is an inexpensive way to have someone design a banner based on your logo and style.

3. Create your own in PowerPoint using a template that you can find at LinkedInBanner.com.

## ✓ PROFILE PICTURE

A high-quality profile headshot is essential. It doesn't matter how much you love your dog, your car, or even the wedding cutout with your spouse's hand on your shoulder—get a professional headshot. People connect with people. Make sure you have a photo where you are smiling and making eye contact—it matters.

### ✓ COVER STORY
Record your thirty-second commercial on the mobile app and upload by clicking on the + on your headshot.

### ✓ HEADLINE (220 CHARACTERS)
Your headline is one of the most valuable real estate places on your profile. Similar to a newspaper, the headline's job is to get your visitors to want to read more. Typically, people have their title and company name but that is not enough to catch your buyer's attention and get them interested in reading further. So, give them something of value. Mention who and how you help and let your buyers know you are speaking directly to their need. Your credibility all starts in your headline.

Mine is:

Transforming the Way Professionals Sell by Converting Connections to Conversations | LinkedIn & Sales Navigator Training | Profile Development | eLearning & Coaching Membership | Host of the Making Sales Social Podcast

### ✓ ABOUT (2600 CHARACTERS)
The goal of your summary is to help influence your stakeholders to want to take your call. That means you need to bring value and resources, not a resume. Although there are many ways to build a powerful summary, here are the six elements all sales professionals need to consider:

1. Open up with a call-to-read. LinkedIn's summary is condensed, so make sure your first line attracts your readers and gets them to click on the "show more" button.

2. Next, talk in a relatable way about your buyers' challenges. Make sure they resonate with the issues you highlighted.

3. Offer insights to get them thinking differently about how they are doing things today. If you can offer value they can implement even if they never have a conversation with you, then you are offering true insights. If the content only works if they work with you, then it's not an insight, it's a pitch.

4. This step is tricky, as you want to be sure that you have laid the groundwork for you to be the vendor of choice without selling them. Give them what they need to know when choosing a vendor and be sure to include your differentiators in that list. In other words, be sure to give them a list of what they need when making this decision and include features and benefits that are unique to your solution.

5. Call-to-action. Okay, now you have their attention. They are curious, but if they don't know what to do now, they will leave your profile and in two minutes forget they ever even found you. Give them a way to raise their hand and say, *"I'd like to learn more."* If you are in sales, ask for the close, which is . . . the call.

6. Make sure you have included your phone number and email.

## ✓ FEATURED

Adding collateral, videos, case studies, and links to articles can all be highlighted in the Summary and Experience sections by adding rich media. By uploading or linking to content relevant to your readers, you can add more credibility to your brand.

Building a value-centric profile is foundational for anyone in a business development role. Take a look at your profile and your content from your clients' perspective and answer these questions: Is it compelling? Does the content create curiosity or get them to think differently? Will it get them excited to take your call?

### ✓ EXPERIENCE (2000 CHARACTERS)

Your job description doesn't have to be a list of your responsibilities. Rather than talking about your years in business, your passion, or your mission, share how you helped your clients. Talk about the difference you made for the people and companies you have worked with.

### ✓ EXPERIENCE HACK (2000 CHARACTERS)

LinkedIn will thread the different positions you hold or held if you are connected to your Company page. While this is meant to list your past roles, you can use this to highlight your deliverables or solutions. This gives you 2000 characters to talk about your offering as well as connecting rich media specific to that offering. You could, in many cases, take content straight from your website.

### ✓ SYMBOLS

Adding symbols to your profile is like "The Three Bears." Papa Bear's profile has nothing—all the words just blend together. Mama Bear's profile is full of fluff, diamonds, crowns, and lots of bling that distracts others from the content. Baby Bear's profile, on the other hand, is just right. He has arrows to draw attention and break up ideas and bullets to create impact around key statements. If you want your profile to pop, visit LinkedInSymbols.com.

## ✓ SKILLS

It is important for your prospects to learn how others see you, so don't be afraid to optimize your content for search engines. This section, in particular, is ideal for search engine optimization (SEO) because it is heavily indexed by Google.

## ✓ EDUCATION

Be sure to add all your educational background even if they are just classes at local schools. This will show your commitment to education, not to mention possibly help in connecting with alumni.

## ✓ RECOMMENDATIONS

A solid testimonial is social proof that you have had an impact on your clients. Identify a few people that you have brought value to over the years, reach out, and have a brief conversation. Let them know you are building your LinkedIn presence and ask if they'd be willing to post a recommendation. You can even offer to write a draft for them to help them get started. Chances are they will use whatever it is that you send them.

Now that your profile is value-centric, there are activities you can do on a daily basis that will convert your LinkedIn connections into conversations on a consistent basis.

## CHECK NOTIFICATIONS

1. Open the LinkedIn app on your desktop.

2. Click on Notifications.

3. Scroll down to the first blue highlighted (unread) messages.

4. Click one at a time and engage appropriately.

5. Mentioned in a post: Click and read the post, like it, and respond to it with a relevant comment.

6. Engagers on your content: Click through and respond to everyone's comments. Don't post and hide! Make sure you engage with everyone who is commenting on your "stuff."

7. Birthdays - I send: Happy Birthday to you♪♫•*¨*•.¸¸ ¸¸.•*¨*•♫♪ Happy Birthday to you ♫♪•*¨*•.¸¸ ¸¸....•*¨*•♫♪Happy Birthday dear @MENTION NAME ♫•*¨*•.¸¸ ¸¸.•*¨*•♫♪ Happy Birthday to you ♫♪•*¨*•.¸¸¸¸.•*¨*•♫♪♫♪•*¨*•.¸¸ ¸¸.•*¨*•♫♪...And MANY MORE!!!♫♫•*¨*•.¸¸

8. New Job: Look at each one and determine whether he or she is someone you just want to congratulate or want to talk to. GENERIC: Congratulations on your new job. With this new role, I am sure you will be getting a lot more profile visitors. I am not sure if you are looking for some ideas to stand out even more. If you are, here is a link to a blog post that may offer some quick tips.

## SEE WHO'S VIEWED YOUR PROFILE

1. Visit Who's Viewed Your Profile.

2. Scan everyone who visited in the last 24 hours.

3. Identify those you want to engage and ignore everyone else.

4. For 1st-degree connections, visit their profile and then send a note:

   • NAME, thanks for visiting my profile. It has been some time since we last connected. May I ask what brought you here today?

5. For those you are not connected to yet, visit their profile, find something you have in common or something worth mentioning and send a connection request:

> NAME, thanks for visiting my profile. I had a chance to visit yours and noticed ABC. If you are open, let's connect. (your name)
>
> P.S. May I ask what brought you to my profile?

## CHECK YOUR MESSAGES

1. Check your Message tab on Mobile.

2. Search for unread messages.

3. First look at new connections that have accepted your LinkedIn connection request and then send them a welcome message that is personal to them. If you connected around content, share other content that relates to that topic or was written by the same creator.

4. Respond to all other messages accordingly.

## MANAGE INVITATIONS

1. Visit the Networking tab on your desktop computer to see if you have any outstanding connection requests.

2. Click on See All.

3. Scan to see all invites with a personal note and either accept and send a welcome message or reply with a message.

4. Welcome note:

Thanks for connecting with me here on LinkedIn.

I am not sure if you are exploring additional ways to leverage LinkedIn for business development, but If you are open, I'd be happy to share some free resources that can help you start more sales conversations by adding value. Let me know—I'll send a link. (your name)

P.S. May I ask how you found me?

5. If you are not sure you want to connect, reply to the message:

Thank you for your connection request, I typically only connect with people I know. May I ask how you found me? (Then ignore. When they respond to your note, you can then accept their connection request or ask them to connect if that option is no longer available.)

## MINE YOUR CLIENT'S CONNECTIONS

1. Prior to a client meeting, I look through their connections.

2. Click on the Search bar.

3. Choose People from the dropdown menu.

4. Click on All Filters.

5. Choose 2nd-degree connections.

6. Type the potential client's name in the Connections Of filter (they must be a 1st-degree connection for this to work).

7. Complete all additional relevant filters.

8. Scroll down to the Title filter and add a search string of your ideal prospects. This is mine: (sales OR marketing) AND ("vice president" OR director).

9. Click Apply All.

**Mine the list and choose 8-10 names**

1. Send the message:

   - Mr. Client, I am so glad we have been able to help solve X for you and your company. I am not sure if you are aware, but the way I have typically grown my business has been from warm introductions from happy clients.

   - I happened to notice that you are connected to eight people on LinkedIn that I'd love to get in front of. Could I run these names by you?"

2. Eventually, move to asking for introductions to the people they know well or get permission to drop their name.

## FIND, SHARE AND ENGAGE ON CONTENT

1. Check three to five people's activities and engage. (Pro-tip: Ring the bell on your prospects profiles so you are notified when they post content.)

2. Look up targeted #hashtags to find new content that is relevant to your audience, learn from it, and add your thought leadership and subject matter expertise in the comments.

3. Capture your genius when you are on calls with clients and prospects and share a tip one to three times a week. Create a post of text content, video, image, or quote to share.

4. Publish a LinkedIn Poll weekly.

5. Leverage LinkedIn LIVE or audio rooms to share your insights weekly.

6. Create quotes from your LIVE in Canva to share throughout the week.

7. Write a weekly or bi-weekly newsletter on LinkedIn.

Brynne Tillman is the LinkedIn Whisperer and CEO of Social Sales Link. For over a decade, she has been teaching Entrepreneurs, sales teams and business leaders how to leverage LinkedIn for social selling.

As a former sales trainer and personal producer, Brynne adopted all of the traditional sales techniques and adapted them to the new digital world. She guides professionals to establish a thought leader and subject matter expert brand, find and engage the right target market, and leverage clients and networking partners to obtain warm introductions that turn into securing qualified buyers.

In addition, Brynne is the co-host of the Making Sales Social podcast and author of *The LinkedIn Sales Playbook, a Tactical Guide to Social Selling*.

Get FREE access to our library of content that carries a wealth of information on LinkedIn and social selling, including on-demand webinars and masterclasses, checklists, and informa-

tional downloads. PLUS! You'll be part of an interactive community of fellow sales professionals.

The job of LinkedIn for social selling is to start more sales conversations without being salesy—and as an entrepreneur, this is vital to growing your business. If you'd like to continue the social selling journey, join our LinkedIn Library as my guest: https://socialsaleslink.com/library.

# Publicity Like A Pro

### CHRISTINA DAVES

As a woman starting out in business, getting visibility for your new venture can be a challenging task. Fortunately, with my Get PR Famous™ Formula, you can learn how to land media coverage and increase your brand's visibility.

The Get PR Famous Formula™ focuses on three key steps: being newsworthy, creating great hooks, and finding the right journalist. By following these steps, you can increase your chances of getting media coverage and reaching your target audience.

## STEP 1 - BEING NEWSWORTHY

Being newsworthy means standing out from the crowd and having a unique angle or perspective that sets you apart from your competitors. As a new business owner, you wonder how to make your brand newsworthy.

One of the most effective ways to make your brand newsworthy is to share your story. Everyone loves a good story. By sharing your story, you can connect with your audience on a personal level. Be sure to highlight what inspired you to start your business and any challenges you've faced along the way. Sharing your story can also help you establish your personal brand and make your business more relatable. Remember, people like to work with people. Story helps you connect.

Another way to be newsworthy is to focus on your unique selling point. What makes your business unique? Whether it's your product, service, brand, your mission, or your approach, be sure to highlight what sets you apart from your competitors. This can help you attract media attention and position your business as a thought leader in your industry.

Newsjacking is another way to make yourself or your business newsworthy. This involves keeping an eye on the news and looking for opportunities to tie your business to current, trending events. See what people are talking about on Google, Twitter, or TikTok. How can you tie yourself into that story and make yourself newsworthy TODAY?

## STEP 2 - CREATING GREAT HOOKS

Creating great hooks means crafting pitches that are attention-grabbing and relevant to a specific journalist and "hooking" them in with your subject line. A great place to look at potential subject lines is magazine covers. These are "hooks" that get you to make an impulse purchase based solely on what's on the cover.

To create great hooks for your actual pitch, you need to think like a journalist. Journalists are always looking for interesting and timely stories to share with their audience. When crafting your pitches, put yourself in their shoes and ask yourself what would make your story stand out. What is the unique angle or perspective that you can bring to the table? How can you make your story relevant to the journalist's audience?

Using studies and statistics is a great way to add credibility to your pitches. By citing research that supports your pitch, you can increase the likelihood that a journalist will take you seriously. You get to ride the coattails of the person or organization who did the research.

Tell a story that will make your pitch more engaging and memorable. Use storytelling techniques to make your pitches more relatable and impactful.

## STEP 3 - FINDING THE RIGHT JOURNALIST

Finding the *right* journalist means doing your research and personalizing your pitches to their interests.

Using Google and social media is a great way to research journalists who cover your industry or niche. Follow them on Twitter or LinkedIn and engage with their content. By getting to know the journalists and their interests, you can craft pitches relevant to their beat.

Reading the journalist's work is also important. By getting a sense of their style and interests, you can tailor your pitches to their preferences. This will increase the likelihood that they will be interested in your story and be willing to cover it.

Building relationships with journalists takes time and effort, but it's worth it. Be respectful of their time and what they cover. Avoid sending generic pitches or spamming them. This could result in them never opening another email from you again.

Building a strong media presence is crucial for any business looking to grow and succeed. It is important to learn how to navigate the media landscape and use it to your advantage. Here are some additional tips to consider when trying to get media coverage for your business:

## USE YOUR UNIQUE PERSPECTIVE AS A FEMALE ENTREPRENEUR

As a female entrepreneur, you have a unique perspective that can set you apart from your male counterparts. Use this to your advantage when crafting your pitches and media outreach.

Share your experiences and insights as a woman in business and highlight how they have influenced your approach to entrepreneurship. This can make your story more compelling and interesting to journalists who are looking for fresh perspectives.

## CONSIDER CONTRIBUTING TO RELEVANT PUBLICATIONS

One way to increase your visibility and establish yourself as an expert in your field is by contributing to relevant publications. Many magazines and online publications are on the lookout for guest contributors who can offer valuable insights and expertise to their readers. Pitch your ideas to these publications and offer to write articles or provide expert commentary. This can be a great way to build your reputation and establish yourself as a thought leader in your industry.

## UTILIZE SOCIAL MEDIA PLATFORMS SUCH AS TWITTER, LINKEDIN, AND INSTAGRAM

These can be powerful tools for reaching journalists and building relationships with them. Follow journalists who cover your industry and engage with their content by sharing and commenting on their posts. You can also use social media to share your own content and promote your business. Make sure to use relevant hashtags and tag relevant publications or journalists to increase your visibility.

If you are successful in landing media coverage, it is important to be prepared for interviews. Make sure you have a clear understanding of the journalist's angle and prepare your talking points in advance. Practice your messaging and be prepared to answer tough questions. Being well-prepared can help you come across as confident and knowledgeable, which can increase your chances of being quoted in the article or featured on the news segment.

Consider reaching out to other female entrepreneurs who have successfully navigated the media landscape. They may be able to offer valuable insights and advice that can help you achieve your goals.

Getting media coverage for your business isn't difficult once you have a strategy. By using the Get PR Famous™ Formula and incorporating these additional tips, you can increase your visibility, establish yourself as an expert in your field, and build your brand. Remember to be newsworthy, create great hooks, and find the right journalist. Utilize your unique perspective as a female entrepreneur, contribute to relevant publications, utilize social media, be prepared for interviews, and don't be afraid to ask for help. With persistence and some effort, you can achieve your media goals and take your business to the next level.

Christina Daves, PR Strategist, is the bestselling author of two books that share her journey of getting exposure for a product she invented.

Having no resources for advertising or the ability to hire a PR firm, Christina taught herself everything she could about generating her own publicity. She has appeared in over 1000 local and national media outlets including: *The Steve Harvey Show, Dr. Oz, TODAY,* local *NBC, ABC, CBS,* and

*FOX,* magazines such as, *Forbes* and *Entrepreneur,* and many more. She regularly appears on local television.

As a result of this success, she launched <u>PR for Anyone</u>® to help other small business owners achieve similar success. Christina is also a keynote speaker, sharing her message inspiring entrepreneurs to gain visibility and credibility through media.

Together with her clients, Christina has over 1 billion views and over $100 million in sales from free publicity.

<u>3StepstoPRSuccess.com</u> – This guide takes you on a deeper dive to the Get PR Famous™ Formula and will help you land in the media today.

*"And the day came when the risk to remain tight in a bud was more painful than the risk it took to blossom."*
ANAÏS NIN, WRITER

# Landing Radio Shows, Virtual Summits and TEDx Events to Attract Clients, Sell Books and Grow Your Business

JACKIE LAPIN

The lifeblood of an entrepreneur is a steady stream of new clients, and the best way to ensure that is to be highly visible where prospective clients will see you.

As a leader, author, coach, or entrepreneur, you must commit time to finding and securing the vehicles that offer visibility, and that includes speaking, podcasts and the three opportunities I will address here: radio shows, virtual summits, and TEDx events. The first task you must undertake is to carve out time in your schedule to get yourself booked for any of these. That means designating a minimum of three hours every week for finding and booking your next visibility opportunity.

So why these three platforms? Most people overlook radio today in the rush to do podcasts, but it's still an incredibly viable medium. Broadcast radio reaches a wide audience—and if you are fortunate enough to get booked for a national show, something syndicated or NPR, that is a home run. Local radio is great for attracting clients and book buyers close to home or supporting a personal appearance or book signing. Besides these shows, you can also pitch yourself to news stations.

If you are going to book yourself for radio, you need to find the producer of a show. A big show will have a dedicated producer. For smaller shows, the host may well be the producer. You want to check out the website or contact the station or network to locate the contact information, especially to find an email and follow-up phone number.

You then want to create a one to one-and-a-half page "pitch letter" that you will email to the host detailing:

- why you should be on their show
- what problem you solve for the audience
- why you are the expert on this subject
- how will you enlighten the listeners
- what impact you will have and what will you speak about during the interview

Send the pitch and follow up by phone to see if you can secure the interview. Also try social media direct messenging for the host or producer if you don't get a response by phone or email. Keep connecting! If it's a solid pitch, someone will say yes and hopefully a lot of someones!

When you go to do these interviews, you will want to provide a media kit to the host so the host can actually support you in connecting with the audience. It should include an overview release about what you are discussing, a full bio, a short four to five paragraph introduction they read when introducing you on the air, twenty questions you want to be asked, and a final page that includes all the links to the ways the public can engage with you—books, social media, products, etc.

The twenty questions are a roadmap that allows you to control the information you want the audience to hear, and induces them into further contact with you. In addition to talking about your mission, services, or book, always offer a free online gift for the audience so you can connect with them after the show. This is the way you monetize radio if you don't get immediate buyers off the show's airing.

Why virtual summits? Virtual summits serve two purposes, they introduce you to prospective clients and book buyers directly, but they also grow your opt-in list so you can begin a relationship with people in an invitational way without sales as a barrier.

Just a quick overview of a summit . . . this is where one host invites multiple "guest presenters" to offer wisdom in a one-hour interview for each. The guest presenter offers a free online informational gift at the end of the talk that encourages people to sign up to get it. All guest presenters promote to their communities—meaning that as a guest presenter, you are exposed to many, many new candidates that you would not otherwise encounter. Summits and online product giveaways are the fastest ways to grow your opt-in list.

To get booked on a summit, assemble the "usual" information into a mini-media kit, a document that includes a three-paragraph biography; title and description of your talk/subject (make it snappy and appealing); the title and description of your enticing gift offering, including the link where to find it; and your social media and website links. You can either send this to a host upon request or use it as a "cheat sheet" when copying the content into an online submission form. One key element in getting booked for these: the host will probably have a theme for the summit. Make sure your subject matter fits with the theme or adapt it specifically for the theme.

Finding summits on your own is a little trickier. Watch for invites to the ones that come in your email inbox and ask to be included in the future. Seek out mastermind colleagues or professional friends to see whom they know. My company, SpeakerTunity, offers a monthly list of summits that are seeking guest presenters. (www.SpeakerTunity.com/summits)

Why TEDx? Local TEDx events are a fantastic showcase that accomplishes many things:

- They enable you to increase your authority and impact.

- They hone your ability to create a powerful message in a short twelve-minute segment (the advertised eighteen minutes actually breaks down to about twelve minutes of delivered content).

- They can expand people's awareness of you and your mission to thousands or even tens of thousands of prospective clients.

- They can open the door to more speaking opportunities.

- Just to name a few!

Local TEDx events are easier to land than national TED TALKS, but that does not mean they are easy to get into! The hosts or judges generally weigh hundreds or more candidates for each event, and they are discriminating about who they choose. One thing you must understand—this is not a selling opportunity! It's only an opportunity to expose attendees to "your idea worth spreading." Anything that is commercial in any nature will be passed over. This is just a showcase opportunity to increase your visibility and build your authority.

You first need to find a TEDx that is ideal for you (and you might have to apply to many!). But local is better because the organizers want to make sure you can get to coaching sessions and rehearsals, so people in proximity are favored over people who live far away. Be prepared to do a two-minute introduction video on your subject and fill out a form with all your key information, including *why you* and a compelling description of your presentation. It can't be generic . . . the title must sell it. And one thing I've heard from the judges consistently— FOLLOW THE DIRECTIONS! If you don't do exactly as they ask, you will be rejected!

Your goal is first to get booked, and secondly to deliver something powerful that will result in a video that has viral potential. But it's important to note that if you want visibility for your TEDx, it is on you to do the promotion. You might get a little help from the promoter, and it will be posted on the national TEDx compendium, but by-and-large, you will need to spread the word. So promote aggressively via email to your community, on social media, in your interviews, though local publicity, etc. Use it in your email signature and on your speaker one-sheet and your speaker proposal letters to get more bookings! Most importantly, it is a great door-opener when you are seeking to introduce yourself to prospective clients.

In summary, radio, virtual summits, and TEDx events all substantially increase your visibility and put you in front of new audiences ripe for what you offer. Your messages must be clear, unique, distinctive, or empowering and show prospects you have a means to improve their lives or businesses—on any of these platforms. Then you must have a method to funnel clients to you once they've been exposed to your message on one of these platforms, and an effective way to get them to go from hello to "yes!"—once they are in the door. That will make your outreach strategy impactful, successful, and enriching for both you and your clients!

Jackie Lapin is the Founder of SpeakerTunity, The Speaker & Leader Resource Company, providing leads, tools, and strategies for leaders, coaches, and entrepreneurs to get booked for speaking engagements, conferences, radio shows, podcasts, virtual summits, TEDx events, and virtual networking. Explore seventy-five regional speaker lead directories, or leads just in your niche all across North America. SpeakerTunity is the Speaker's Ultimate Toolbox, one-stop-shopping for the speaker. Check out SpeakerTunity's new membership program: Member's Only! www.SpeakerTunity.com.

Free Gift: 44 Ways To Seduce Your Next Client from Stage, Podcast, Radio, Virtual Summits, and Virtual Networking—44 different type types of opt-in lead magnets that will prove irresistible to audiences  when delivered from any platform! www.SpeakerTunity.com/seduce

*You can design and create and build the most wonderful*
*place in the world. But it takes people to make*
*the dream a reality.*
WALT DISNEY

# 5 Steps To Affordable & Efficient Delegation In Your Business

BROOK BORUP

Are you struggling to keep up with the demands of your business?

Do you find yourself overwhelmed by the amount of work that needs to be done on a daily basis?

Do you wish you could find affordable help; help that can also do things the way you would do them?

If so, it's time to take a step back and gain clarity in your business to determine the areas where you require assistance. By doing this, you can acquire affordable support that will help streamline your operations and boost productivity.

Acquiring affordable support for your small business can be a daunting task, especially when you don't know where to start. Here are some pro tips on how to plan for the delegation your small business needs:

## STEP 1: RECORD YOUR DAILY ACTIVITIES

To understand your business's specific needs, keep track of all the tasks you perform regularly. Much like a lawyer keeping notes for billing, this log will help you identify how much time you spend on each task and which ones you can delegate to someone else. This could include data entry, email management, social media scheduling, or appointment setting.

If you have ever worked with a personal trainer to lose weight or get in shape, the dreaded food log is, in my opinion, the worst part. This is where you need to suck it up because it *will* help you succeed. Do this log for ten days and keep detailed notes and I guarantee you will be able to create a plan to delegate forty percent of the time you are currently spending on your business.

## STEP 2: DREAM OF THE POSSIBILITIES

Now that you have a list of where your time goes, it's time to put these tasks into three categories using three different color highlighters or marking tools of your choice.

### *CATEGORY ONE–WHAT COULD BE TEMPLATED, AUTOMATED, OR MADE EASIER?*

You may not have any idea about software or systems but that is okay this category will just be a bit light in tasks. Typically, when we are working with a small business owner we can put about forty percent of your current tasks into this category. This allows you to let the software do the work, so you only need to invest money in the setup.

### *CATEGORY TWO–WHAT COULD I TEACH SOMEONE ELSE TO DO?*

This is the delegation category. If you can write down a process, do a video showing someone how you like it, or you just hate doing it, then it can be delegated at some point in the future. This does not mean you have to delegate it all to one person, it just means you can work on yourself to let it go because it doesn't require your brain.

## CATEGORY THREE–ONLY MY BRAIN OR SPECIAL SKILLS CAN COMPLETE THIS TASK FROM BEGINNING TO END

For most of us this usually boils down to the thing we sell and the sales process for it. This includes taking your client meetings, sales meetings, etc.

Now start marking up your list.

**Pro-tip:** You might find, for example, when you send a proposal it takes four to five steps. Think about those steps. If you had a process, all you would have to do is the scope of work and someone else could do the rest—including following up on the proposal.

## STEP 3: BUILD OUT TASKS AND JOB DESCRIPTIONS

Once you've identified the tasks that can be delegated, create a job description (or several) and determine the type of person you need to hire to fill that role. This information will help you choose the right candidate when you have the funds to hire and grow. Additionally, think about specialized skills that would benefit your company but may not require full-time employment. For example, graphic design or website maintenance may only be needed periodically and each may require special skills.

**Pro-tip:** Most people who are going to work for you are not skilled in all the areas. You may need to hire four people for ten to twenty hours a week in order to get all your tasks delegated and done correctly the first time.

## STEP 4: DEVELOP TRAINING ON "YOUR WAY" OF COMPLETING TASKS

You need to understand how to do each of the tasks you ask someone to do for you. If you are doing them yourself now, then this is as easy as documenting each task as you do it the next time. You can use tools like Scribe, Loom, and Berrycast to create standard operating procedures (SOPs) on how to complete specific tasks so you can easily delegate to your future team.

**Pro-tip:** Efficient software systems and processes are essential to streamline your business operations. Using software like ActiveCampaign and QuickBooks Online (QBO) can help automate some tasks so you can supplement your delegation budget and have a more robust business process.

## STEP 5: NOW YOU CAN FIND THE RIGHT PEOPLE TO HIRE

At this point, you have probably put in about twenty to forty hours of solid work to understand your business needs on a fundamental level. This is not an easy task if you are not used to thinking proactively about the needs of your business. You should have clarity on the skills required of the person you want to hire, the personality type that will suit your working style, and what will be expected of them when they are hired.

In addition to the required skills, hiring someone who aligns with your values and work culture can lead to a more productive and happy work environment. Therefore, consider what kind of person you want to work with and cater to their needs.

Before hiring anyone, you need to know what they will do for you and how you will measure their performance. Understanding the role helps you identify the skills and experience required to perform it successfully. It's important to set clear expectations with your team from the beginning to make sure your future team members fully understand their role and responsibilities.

**Pro-tip:** Hire everyone on a thirty- to sixty-day trial basis. If you have done the work above, they should be able to jump in and catch on quickly. Please remember that some jobs take skill and require a higher rate of pay, but not all tasks and skills are equal in value or the time it takes to learn the skill. Hire based on the resume, the interview, and your gut. Having all these things in place will set you both up for success. If the new hire is not a right fit, fire fast and find someone new.

## GET CLARITY ON WHAT YOU'RE SELLING

To enable others to do what you do, you need to be clear about what you're selling and who your target audience is. This clarity will enable you to teach others to sell your product or service efficiently.

## BE A MANAGER AND LEADER

Virtual assistants (VAs) are task-oriented and will complete tasks the way you instruct them. As a manager and leader, it's essential to delegate tasks effectively and provide clear instructions. Use task managers to help your VAs complete tasks efficiently and communicate regularly with your team. Schedule regular check-ins, provide feedback on performance, and listen actively to ideas and suggestions. This will help them feel valued and invested in the success of your business.

## PAY FOR CRITICAL THINKING AND PROBLEM-SOLVING SKILLS

Although you may be looking for affordable support, it's essential to invest in individuals who can think critically and solve problems. Such individuals are valuable and can help your business grow. Offer opportunities for growth within your company. Whether it's through additional training or advancement opportunities, giving virtual assistants a chance to develop their skills can lead to long-term loyalty.

To wrap up, acquiring affordable support for your small business is possible by following these steps with a little help from the *pro-tips*. However, it's essential to understand your business needs and invest in people who can add value to your business.

The power of implementing scalable systems and processes in your business leads to a profitable business with a team that provides you with the ultimate dream of absentee ownership.

 Brook Borup is the Architect and Business Builder behind the Done-For-You Agency My Clone Solution (myclonesolution.com) and Founder of The Small Business Growth Community (smallbusinessgrowth.org). Brook's goal is to keep small business owners in business. She's seen enough owners have to make the hard choice between their kids' little league game or more hours in their business to keep the mortgage paid. She understands that the stakes are higher because every penny spent on a product or service could be food on the table or the family vacation they haven't had in years. My Clone Solution was founded on Brook's vision that everyone deserves help. Brook and her loyal team of Clones strive to make this a reality every single day.

Get help implementing these tips for your specific business needs by scheduling a free twenty-two-minute call today at **myclonesolution. com**! You'll have Brook's undivided attention to get you started down the right path of automating your business and lightening your workload.

Our twenty-two-minute free call is called Ask Anything for three good reasons. We can save you money, time, or give you a connection that will help. The only goal is to help and that is priceless. https://call.myclonesolution.com

*"As I often lecture businesses, it is not the email you
send which matters, but how people
feel when they read it."*
KATIE HOPKINS

# Increasing Your Income with Email

ELLEN FINKELSTEIN

You've probably heard that you need to build your list of subscribers, but once you have the first person on that list, what do you do?

Many entrepreneurs leave their subscribers hanging and don't email them for days, weeks, or even months.

Why is that, when they know email marketing is such an important way for them to make money?

Here are a number of reasons I've heard from clients and colleagues. Maybe . . .

1.  You don't know what to write. Maybe you don't have anything to sell yet, or you have only one product and you don't want to sell it over and over.

2.  You can't find the time (each email takes you quite a bit of time) or you're too busy doing other things in your business.

3.  You worry that people will unsubscribe.

Can you relate to any of these?

I'll respond to those three objections . . .

## 1. YOU DON'T KNOW WHAT TO WRITE

Once you have a structure for your emails, you'll always have something to write—something that will be interesting and valuable to your subscribers.

There's a simple formula for the types of content you can send your subscribers:

### EDUCATION

This includes tips strategy, techniques, etc. People are hungry to learn. If you have a blog (which I recommend), you can send a short email linking to the post. Or just give them a short tip.

**Bonus Tip:** Recycle older blog posts.

**Bonus Tip:** Write your tips for the month all at one time and then send them out throughout the month.

### INSPIRATION

Your subscribers want you to inspire them! They need inspiration to take action. They need to hear that they can get the results they want. You can do this with stories from your own experience, stories from your clients (case studies), quotes from well-known people, and just by being uplifting.

**Bonus Tip:** Collect quotes you like, collect case studies from your clients, and tell micro stories from your daily life. You can connect almost anything to a message that's relevant to your audience.

### OFFERS

There are two problems people have with making offers.

- **Some entrepreneurs are afraid to make offers.** They think selling will turn off their subscribers. The opposite is true. Think of your offers as resources for your subscribers—because they are. You can't give people everything they need to succeed within your emails. People need to go deeper and they do that with courses, coaching, etc. You need to make offers in order to help your subscribers get results. If you don't, you're letting them down.

- **Some entrepreneurs have nothing to offer.** Maybe you don't have products or services yet. Yes, you need to create those. But until then, find other people's products to promote. You can find an unlimited number of products to promote as an affiliate or from some other type of partnership. Again, if you aren't doing this, you are not serving your subscribers well.

**Bonus Tip:** Don't think you have to make a BIG product. You can make a fifteen-minute video and sell it at a low price. You can combine a few blog posts into an eBook. You can interview some experts and package that as a product.

**Bonus Tip:** Educate as you sell. Tell people *why* they should buy. Your subscribers will thank you for the education.

You need to train your subscribers to click. This means you always need at least one link. Your strategy should be to get people interested and then provide a link.

## 2. YOU CAN'T FIND THE TIME

There are three reasons you may not find the time to send out emails:

- You aren't prioritizing your emails

- You're too busy doing other things

- Your emails take you too much time

You might misunderstand the place that emails have in your business. Email is the most powerful way to earn an income from your subscribers. It's true that there are other powerful ways to earn an income, like selling on a webinar or live event, but most people get to those events via email. Email is the starting point. Make it a priority.

Again, if you're too busy doing other things, you need to reconfigure your day. Write your email as the first thing you do in the morning. Let's say you give yourself from 9 am to 10 am each morning to write an email. Block that off on your calendar so you don't have any appointments during that time. It's important to add writing emails as a calendar item each morning.

After that, you have the rest of your day to do other things.

If your emails take you more than an hour, you're spending too much time on them. Keep them short. Recycle content from the previous email. Work from your list of tips and quotes that you've collected. If you're promoting others as an affiliate, keep a list of people to promote and watch for emails asking you to promote. Put these items on your calendar, too.

When emails are hard, you don't write them, so make them easy.

**Bonus Tip:** If you prefer to write in the afternoon or evening, schedule your emails for the next morning.

Being consistent and persistent with your emails will help you develop a group of loyal subscribers.

## 3. YOU WORRY THAT PEOPLE WILL UNSUBSCRIBE

Don't! Just give people valuable information on the topic you promised. Be consistent. And continually grow your list.

Unsubscribes will always happen. Some of those are people who will never buy from you. Others just don't relate to your approach. This is part of email marketing. Get over it.

### CONSIDER A NEWSLETTER TYPE OF EMAIL

Conventional wisdom says that each newsletter should have only one call to action, but that can seem very commercial to your subscribers.

Consider a newsletter type of email, which has multiple clickable resources, whether they are educational, inspirational, or commercial—usually a combination of these.

Why? Because there's something for everyone in each email. For example, you can include a story, a tip, an affiliate link, and an offer of your own program in one email. People will look forward to seeing what you have for them, take what they want, and leave what they don't want.

In addition, because you can promote an offer multiple times without devoting an entire email to it, you can promote more often than other entrepreneurs. In my experience, this can get you better results than people with much larger lists. I have often done better on affiliate joint ventures than people with lists that are four to ten times the size of mine.

So, it's a win for you *and* a win for your subscribers.

### WHAT'S NEXT?

As soon as you have a single subscriber, get in the habit of emailing regularly with a wide variety of content. And be sure to include offers, because, after all, you're in business!

Ellen Finkelstein teaches online entrepreneurs how to get their knowledge out to the world, including how they can maximize their income with email marketing.

During her twenty-plus years online, Ellen has successfully created and sold dozens of online products and courses. She uses her experience to help others turn their knowledge into online products so they can transform others.

Ellen has become well known for her contrarian and wildly successful email newsletter formula, which she uses to rank highly on affiliate leaderboards and gain clients for her own coaching and training business.

It isn't hard to improve the results you get from emails, so I'd like to offer you a free guide, "10 Techniques for Better Results from Your Emails." Just implement these ideas, one by one, and you'll see your profits grow!

https://www.ellenhelps.me/10techniques-emailcourse

*"People will forget what you said, people will forget what you did, but people will never forget how you made them feel."*
MAYA ANGELOU

# Public Speaking for Business

### LEISA REID

Would you like to make a bigger impact in your business?

Guess what! *Speaking* is one of the easiest ways to attract your ideal clients!

Below I've outlined some of the top strategies to help you *get* booked and *stay* booked as a speaker, whether you're just getting started or are already a seasoned speaker.

Over the years, I've booked over 600 talks, and learned a lot on my journey.

Back in 2013, I had zero speaking gigs (0 clients, 0 email list, 0 speaking gigs)!

Within my first year as a speaker, I booked eighty-three speaking gigs, filled ten workshops, and attracted hundreds of clients.

People asked me how did I get those kinds of results. That's when "Get Speaking Gigs Now" was born and I started sharing The Speaker's Attraction Formula with people like you.

The tips I'm sharing with you are *real* tips I still use today to get booked and stay booked as a speaker. I like to keep it fun, simple, and strategic.

## TIP #1: THE SECRET TO A STEADY STREAM OF SPEAKING REFERRALS

### *FIND YOUR SPEAKER SOULMATE!*
**What is a Speaker Soulmate?**

Back in 2013, I was exhausted from cold calling and going it alone. I realized it could be easier if I had a partner, so I found someone who spoke at about the same frequency as I did. I trusted and liked her, and she spoke to the same audiences, but wasn't my competition. I shared my plan with her and we started collaborating.

My Speaker Soulmate and I have since referred hundreds of speaking engagements to each other where the red carpet is rolled out, making cold calling rare. Without this collaborative relationship, we would both be cold calling, exhausted, and getting a lot more no's than yes's.

The people in my Speaker's Training Academy develop their own speaker soulmate system to make finding speaking gigs easy and fun, *not* filled with a ton of cold calls and rejections.

Imagine getting an email with the subject heading, we want you! That's what happened to me recently due to a referral made by my speaker soulmate.

Wouldn't you like to get an email with the "we want you!" as a speaker in the subject line?

*To Recap:*

**A Speaker Soulmate is someone who:**

1. Speaks at a similar frequency as you

2. You know, like, and trust

3. Speaks to similar audiences, but is *not* your competition

**YOUR ACTION STEPS:**

- List three people who might be potential speaker soulmates.

- Set up a meeting to see if they want to exchange speaking referrals.

- If you get a *yes*, schedule a time to exchange speaking referrals!

## TIP #2: TWO SPEAKER STRATEGIES TO ATTRACT YOUR IDEAL CLIENTS

### STRATEGY #1 - SHARE HOW YOU SOLVE PROBLEMS

When you are speaking, whether it is for thirty seconds or sixty minutes, it's important to make it valuable for the audience. As a business owner, you also want to attract the types of people you can truly help. One of the most effective ways to do this is to share how you solve problems.

For example:

- I teach entrepreneurs how to get their talk ready to rock so they know what to say and what to offer on stage.

- I teach entrepreneurs how to grow their businesses through speaking without a ton of cold calling.

So, what problems do *you* solve?

## STRATEGY #2 - TELL A STORY ABOUT HOW YOU SOLVE PROBLEMS

Now that you have a list of how you solve problems, we're going to super-size this tip so you attract your ideal clients. The next step is to share how you solve problems by telling a *story* about how you did it.

For example:

- Laura came to me with too many ideas and couldn't narrow her talk down. We created her talk *and* decided what would be the best offer she could give from the stage that would grow her business. She has never sold from stage before and now knows exactly how she is going to do it.

- Mike knew in his heart and soul that speaking was the best way for him to grow his business, but he didn't have any idea about how to get booked. He didn't go on social media, didn't network, and didn't want to cold call. Through working together, he was able to book three speaking gigs through some simple strategies. He was amazed that it worked and people said *yes*!

So, what stories can *you* share that would highlight how you solve people's problems?

**Hint:** Think of clients you've helped or awesome results you've seen from your products/services.

## TIP #3: THE FIRST 3 KEYS TO THE SPEAKER'S ATTRACTION FORMULA

### KEY #1 - GET YOUR TALK READY TO ROCK

If you don't have a talk ready to go, it is difficult (and stressful) to get booked as a speaker. You *must* put your stake in the ground and decide what you stand for.

The template expert speakers use to get booked:

- Title (attractive, clear)

- Description (a brief synopsis of what your talk is going to deliver)

- Learning Points (what will the audience learn/ take away)

### KEY #2 - CREATE YOUR IDEAL SPEAKING GIG PIPELINE

A Speaking Gig Pipeline is a prospect list for speaking gigs where you will get clear on your ideal prospective speaking gigs.

Start thinking about *where* you would ideally want to speak. *Who* would you want in the audience? *What* do you need to have in place to reach out to the organizer(s) so you shine and have your confidence at an all-time high?

### KEY #3 - MONETIZE YOUR SPEAKING

When people work closely with me, they share their obstacles around money and asking for the sale. They want to give so much that they forget to be open to receiving and allowing the natural flow of exchange (of goods and services) to occur.

Can you relate to giving a TON and sometimes forgetting to receive?

Allow me to show you the possibilities available when you utilize speaking to grow your business by walking you through my handy-dandy Speaker's Monetization Formula. This allows you to begin creating a vision for how speaking can grow your business.

## SPEAKERS' MONETIZATION FORMULA

The Speaker Monetization Formula consists of three main variables.

1. Price of your product/service

2. # of gigs/year you ideally want to have

3. # of clients you imagine you could attract per gig

Allow yourself to dream big here and imagine what this would look like for you. I understand that this exercise might be tricky—you might experience some resistance. It's ok. Just allow yourself to dream a little and write down the numbers that pop into your mind.

**Step 1:** What is your favorite or most popular product or service? How much do you charge for it? Write that number down.

**Step 2:** How many speaking gigs do you see yourself having each year?

**Step 3:** How many clients do you think you would retain at each gig?

**Total up your numbers by multiplying them together.** You should have a dollar amount that is very healthy! If not, then perhaps there are some adjustments to be made in your pricing or you might be leaving money on the table that you're not seeing. That's where having expert guidance can be a fast pass to the front of the line!

By now, you have learned a lot! You probably have some notes that are getting you excited about the prospect of sharing your message and transforming many lives! All while having fun and growing your business at the same time.

Below are the questions you can complete to crystallize what you've learned and set you up for success as a speaker.

WHO will you reach out to in the next week to exchange speaking referrals?

1.

2.

3.


What PROBLEMS do you solve for people in your business?

1.

2.

3.


What STORIES can you tell about the problems you solve?

1.

2.

3.

**Fill in your own numbers to the Speaker's MONETIZATION Formula (use your imagination—dream!)**

1. Your Product/Service Price: $_____

2. # of Speaking Gigs in a year: _____

3. # of Clients you think you'll get at each Gig: _____

Total Speaker Sales Potential (multiply the top 3 #'s to get this answer) $_____

In conclusion, I hope you are pumped up and ready to go *rock it* as a speaker! After speaking to hundreds of audiences over the years, I can confidently say there are people who can benefit from your expertise. Your knowledge may be the very solution they are looking for to solve their problems.

There are more than enough opportunities for you to speak, especially now! Make the minor adjustments needed to increase your confidence and success as a virtual speaker so you can continue to make the impact you were born to make.

Do you want to be a speaker, but aren't sure what to talk about, where to go to find gigs, or how to offer your services from stage? As the Founder of Get Speaking Gigs Now, Leisa mentors professionals who want to use public speaking to grow their business. Clients who work closely with her build their speaking skills and confidence through the Speaker's Training Academy. They get their "Talks Ready to Rock" and learn how to stay booked as speakers through easy to implement strategies. As a speaker herself, Leisa has successfully booked and delivered over 600 speaking engagements. In her book, *Get Speaking Gigs Now*, she shares her 7 Step System to Getting Booked, Staying Booked & Attracting Your Ideal Clients Through Speaking.

To learn more visit: https://GetSpeakingGigsNow.com

Get **5 Top Tips to Get More Speaking Gigs** @ https://GetSpeakingGigsNow.com/tips

# Shy Guide to Self-Promotion

## KAT STURTZ

H ello. My Name is Kat.

I'm a smart, mature woman with a quick wit and quirky nature. It's taken me a while to embrace that inner side of me. To let it shine, not just sometimes when in the company of close friends and family, but in conference rooms full of business folks I've never met before. Individuals whose prestige and celebrity are well known. People who light up a room when entering, a smile on their face, full of poise and confidence.

I'm eager to meet them, to shake their hands, to engage in conversations that go deeper than *Hi. Nice to meet you.*

My plans include some serious networking, with vibes on full alert for finding and attracting potential new clients and business peers open to the potential of creating mutually rewarding projects together.

But first I've got to settle my nerves. I look down at my belly, focusing on the butterflies swarming erratically inside.

*Please*, I beg of them. *It's time to settle down. Fly in formation a while. We're in this together and I need you to help me shine. Nothing bold or glaring. A warm welcoming glow will do.*

**Consider yourself warned.**

What I'm about to share may not be what you were expecting. There are no secrets promising to help you suddenly come out of your shy shell, brimming with confidence.

No simple step-by-step to-dos that claim will eradicate your shyness, morph you into a social butterfly, and solve all your speaking in public qualms or nervous one-on-one business chats.

No calls to *just do it*. Because willpower alone won't get it done. Sorry Nike.

No, this advice may not be what you were expecting. And that's by conscious design. You see, one of the most important things I discovered in 1984 while writing my first book (using the byline Kathy Henderson) was that even though my book was similar to others already on the market, it was also different. Unique in some ways.

After weeks of trying to pigeon-hole my concept into the well-established industry norm, I said *screw it.* I decided to put it together my way and if it didn't sell, I'd try something else or just chuck it.

Long story short, the first edition of *Market Guide for Young Writers* not only sold well, but it also earned a few awards and launched my speaking career. Writer's Digest Books, the first publisher to reject my manuscript, later contracted with me to publish the last four editions as *The Young Writer's Guide to Getting Published.*

It was a total surprise to have the editor-in-chief admit one day that they liked some of the unique elements of my book so much they incorporated them into their own annual edition of *Writer's Market*.

## So, what's the point?

The point is being different and true to yourself is just one way to switch on that inner light within you.

As Oscar Wilde said, "Be yourself; everyone else is already taken."

However, that success didn't turn me into a confident, brightly shining extrovert.

Yes, I did go on to enjoy giving presentations in many schools. And I managed fairly respectable presentations for larger audiences at writer's conferences and industry association conventions, like the National Council of Teachers of English and the American Book Sellers Association.

But even now it's a continuing journey of deliberate choices to muster the butterflies, be open to opportunities, accept the challenges, and shine despite the internal urge to self-sabotage.

## Most who know me now assume I'm an extrovert. I'm not.

I spent all of my childhood, teens, and young adult life as an introvert. There are a few vivid memories where I recall boldly stepping out of the shadows and into the limelight, anxious to be seen and heard as a leader rather than quietly following along, only to be shot down and put in my place. Sometimes on purpose by a bully. But impressions are more often about well-meaning adults seeking to guard my timid, sensitive nature, evident by my always-the-good-girl demeanor.

Still the result was the same. I stayed safe and protected, hiding in the shadows. Wanting something more, to be something more, to live more comfortably and confidently in my own skin. To choose to shine when and where I pleased.

**What I want for you: I want you to shine as only you can.**

There's an inner light in each of us just waiting to be switched on.

I want you to respect and honor your inner light, your unique personality. I want you to be able to confidently choose when and where to share your talents, gifts, insights, and innovations.

I want your inner light to glow like a beacon, helping those who are most in need or want of your products, services, and presence to be able to more easily find you, connect with you, buy from you, hire you.

You already know you can't do that hiding in the shadows. I'm not expecting you to change who you are. I want you to value who you are.

I want you to face your fears about shining your inner light so others can see it and be drawn to you like a moth to a flame.

Understand that no one can choose to flip your inner light on but you. You're in control. Well, there's those dang internal butterflies, but you'll need to discover your own way to deal with the persistent, pesky little pests.

You can try sweet talking them into submission, however, I've found the best approach is to be polite yet firm. Let them enjoy their willy-nilly fluttering before and after a spotlight event. Trust them to come through for you when you most need their cooperation.

Just so you know, I fully admit still failing miserably at times in the shining light department.

There isn't a once and done behavior modification transformation. It's about taking responsibility for your entrepreneurial dreams and what it will take to make them come true.

I want you to be willing to choose your moments to shine. Self-promotion requires it.

**You're in charge of the switch.**

No one, and certainly no article or book, can make you shine if you refuse to do your part. *No one* . . . absolutely *no one* can make you stand up and stand out, to be fully focused on the spotlight lit from within. Even if you have the means to hire a full-fledged PR and publicity agency who *could* conceivably get others to focus a spotlight on you, they can't reach your inner light switch unless you agree. Unless *you* make a conscious choice to shine in the moment.

And if somehow they *did* turn you on from the inside without your agreement, that means they, or someone else, could also pull your plug anytime they pleased. Worse, you'd likely burn out from within. It's so heartbreaking when that happens to others. Don't let it happen to you.

I love this quote from Dolly Parton:

"Being a star just means that you just find your own special place, and that you shine where you are. To me, that's what being a star means."

**Are you really an introvert?**

Maybe. Maybe not. Just maybe you're something else. Something better and different, like I discovered about myself.

I'm an ambivert. Simply put, that's someone who occasionally acts less shy and fearful than an introvert, but who is not as consistently bold and outgoing as an extrovert.

We tend to believe our natural tendencies are pre-determined at birth. But honestly, isn't it true that too often we let what others say about us—and what "society" says is true—color not only our beliefs but our emotions and actions as well?

I believe many of us who have always believed ourselves to be shy *introverts* naturally lacking in self-confidence are actually *ambiverts* who can *choose* to adapt and shine in select social and spotlight situations.

**Woohoo!**

What could be more liberating than choosing to be an introvert on purpose? And also recognizing that we can selectively choose our moments to shine!

That's welcome news when you consider it's next to impossible to effectively promote yourself and your business when you keep your inner light dimmed and barely visible to the naked eye.

If I wasn't an ambivert all along, then somewhere between then and now, I became one.

Perhaps you are, too, and just haven't realized it yet.

Honor that light switch inside you. It has a purpose. Use it.

I'm looking forward to seeing how and when you choose to let your inner light shine bright on the entrepreneurial frontier.

Kat is a business life mentor, speaker, award-winning nonfiction author, and The Purgatory Relief Coach for People Who Think Marketing Is Hell (her preferred term as seasoned Certified Guerrilla Marketing Coach).

Her passion is helping home-based solopreneurs and small business owners identify what really has them stumped, stuck, or stalled so they can rock their unique path to success. She especially loves helping time and cash-strapped solopreneurs who work from home move past the obstacles that keep them trapped in despair and leaking money or making little at all.

She runs 56 Vibes Services, RockingYourPath.com, and YouCanCuisine.com (with her retired chef hubby) offering courses, services, and private and group coaching from their home office in rural Michigan.

Despite fighting shyness, overwhelm, frustration, and being downright stuck and scared at times, she's always found a way to clear her path and start moving forward again.

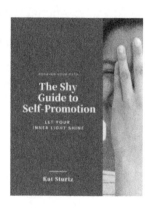

Stop hiding. It's time to let your inner light shine so you can rock your unique path to success. Access a free copy and more at https://rockingyourpath.com/shy-guide-special

*"Great things are done by a series of small things brought together."*
VINCENT VAN GOGH

# The Power Of Microproducts

CHAD ELJISR

Have you ever spent countless hours creating a big project, only to find that it didn't bring in the returns you were hoping for? As an online entrepreneur, I found myself in this exact situation more than once.

I would invest time, money, and effort into researching, creating, and marketing online training programs and courses, hoping to see a return on my investment. However, despite my best efforts, sometimes my offer didn't bring in the number of buyers I'd hoped to attract.

Don't get me wrong, the eLearning industry is exploding, and my business was thriving, but something happened that changed everything for me.

In March 2020, when the pandemic hit, my focus was on selling high-ticket coaching and training programs to clients. However, as the world changed and businesses strived to keep up, I found myself struggling to attract new clients and make sales. It was clear something needed to change, and that's when I decided to pivot my business and focus on creating and selling microproducts.

It was a test. I didn't have all the answers. But what happened next made me completely change my business model to one that helped me build a recession-proof, low-hassle, high-profit, and highly predictable business.

Before I go further, you might wonder, what's a microproduct?

A microproduct is a digital product that is easy and fast to create, comes with a high perceived value, and has a price tag between $7 and $47.

It's also limited in its scope, resolving one very specific problem. Ideally, it's a solution that will help your customer get an explicit result while saving time or money.

The product itself can be content based, a collection of useful assets, or tools. Let's take a look at some specific examples of digital microproducts that you can easily create and sell:

1) **Short Reports:** Short reports are a great way to provide targeted value to your audience on a specific topic. These can be created in a matter of hours and can be sold as a standalone product or used as a lead magnet to attract new subscribers to your email list.

2) **Quick Video Tutorials:** Video tutorials are a highly engaging and effective way to provide value to your audience. They can be created using free or low-cost software and can be sold as a standalone product or used as part of a larger offering.

3) **Checklists and Action Guides:** Checklists and action guides are useful tools for helping your audience to take action on a specific topic. These can be created in a matter of hours and can be sold as a standalone product or used as a bonus to incentivize customers to purchase a larger offering.

4) **Business Templates:** Business templates are a great way to provide value to your audience by helping them streamline their business processes. These can include templates for things like business plans, marketing plans, and financial projections.

5) **Fill-In-The-Blank Swipe Files:** A swipe file is a collection of marketing and copywriting examples to use for inspiration. Swipe files are a useful tool for helping your audience create effective marketing materials. These can include templates for things like email subject lines, blog post titles, and social media posts.

6) **Useful Rolodexes** covering a specific niche: A useful Rolodex can provide valuable information and resources for your audience. These can include things like lists of recommended tools and resources or contact information for experts in a specific field.

7) **White Label Content:** White label content can provide high-quality content for your audience without having to create it from scratch. This can include things like articles, blog posts, and social media content.

8) **Done-For-You Social Media Graphics:** Social media graphics are an important part of any online marketing strategy. By creating and selling pre-designed graphics, you can provide value to your audience and help them create engaging social media content quickly and easily.

9) **White Label Niche Planners:** Niche planners are a useful tool for helping your audience organize and plan their business activities. By creating and selling pre-designed niche planners, you can provide targeted

value to your audience and help them achieve their business goals.

For example, if we decided to create "A List Of Useful Resources" to sell, it could easily be a rolodex of recommended Fiverr.com outsourcing gigs for content creators, a list of top high-ticket affiliate products to promote, etc.

One of the biggest advantages of microproducts is they allow you to test the market quickly and easily. Because they are small and targeted, you can create them based on your knowledge of your audience and what they need, then put them out into the world to see how they are received. This means you can fail and move forward quickly, without risking too much of your time or resources.

In fact, minimizing risk is one of the biggest benefits of microproducts. By keeping your investment of time and resources low, you can experiment and try out new ideas without worrying about the potential for failure. And if a microproduct doesn't perform as well as you hoped, you can simply move on to the next one without having lost too much in the process.

Another advantage of microproducts is that they are incredibly versatile. You can repurpose them in your sales funnel in a variety of ways, from using them as lead magnets to offering them as bonuses to customers who purchase higher-end products. You can even bundle multiple microproducts together to create a more comprehensive offer.

The whole idea is this: microproducts get the *customers*. While back-end offers generate *profits*. The goal of microproducts is to get as many targeted customers as possible into your sales funnel.

Once you have a customer, you can build the know, like, and trust factor, and then offer back-end products that are higher priced and more complex. Back-end products include courses, coaching programs, and other high-ticket items that generate profit for your business.

These back-end products are designed to provide in-depth training and support to customers who are committed to achieving their goals. They require more time and effort to create than microproducts, but they also provide a much higher return on investment. Back-end products are typically sold to customers who have already purchased a microproduct or have otherwise demonstrated a high level of interest in your offers.

Here's my formula for creating small, fast-to-produce and easy-to-sell digital products that helped me build a multi-six-figure business:

1) I launch eight to twelve microproducts per year. This is how I build my list of *buyers*. A microproduct launch brings between 200 and 600 new customers. That's around 4,000 new *buyer* leads in one year. I leverage affiliates, as well as social media, to get traffic to my offers.

2) I created a portfolio of "premium products" selling them for between $97 and $297. I market those premium products directly to my buyer's list.

3) I promote quality products that I believe are useful for my target audience. That's called affiliate marketing. That's an easy way to add at least twenty percent to my income, just by leveraging my buying audience.

4) I create and sell low-cost products that sell directly to my list, with no affiliate sales. This time I am selling to my list of buyers. It is not a moneymaker, but strategically it is important. A lot of people add

value with free access to different products. I don't, for a specific reason: the perceived value is almost never done with "free." At the same time, for just a few dollars, my audience can access high-value training, resources, or tools, and this will boost the trust and authority of my personal brand.

5) I offer my done-for-you product-creation services. I help people by creating their digital product for them, their funnel, etc. Those services start at $1,500.

6) I offer coaching services. I provide my customers with business clarity, a customized online strategy, implementation, technical support, and an accelerated path to building their online biz. There are different packages, from $97 to $9,000.

That's it. Do the math, and you will see how it all adds up.

I am sharing what I do so you can model the above steps and adapt them to your own business.

One of the key benefits of creating microproducts is the compound effect they can have on your business over time. By consistently creating and selling microproducts, you can build up a library of valuable resources that can be repurposed and combined into larger training programs.

For example, I found that by creating a microproduct every four to six weeks, I was able to sell them and discover what was working with my audience. I could then use this feedback to refine and improve my approach, creating even better microproducts in the future.

And then, after six to ten months, I would take several of these microproducts and combine them into a full-fledged training program. By doing this, I was able to leverage the work I had already done and turn it into a more comprehensive and valuable offering.

This approach allowed me to avoid the pitfalls of spending months creating a training program without any income or feedback. Instead, I was able to test and refine my ideas in real-time, building a library of valuable resources that I could use to create even more value for my customers.

If you are looking to build a successful online business, I encourage you to explore the power of microproducts. By consistently creating and selling these small but valuable offerings, you can build a loyal audience, establish yourself as an expert in your field, and lay the groundwork for even greater success in the future.

Chad Eljisr is a serial entrepreneur who created and sold seven businesses, ranging from magazine and book publishing to event organization.

He was the first person to introduce big business gurus such as Jay Conrad Levinson, Jack Trout, Jeff Gitomer, and Tom Peters into the Eastern European market.

In 1999, he founded an internet media company, which he sold to an investment fund for seven figures in 2007.

Today, Chad runs a location-independent business from his laptop focused on helping entrepreneurs leverage their knowledge and expertise to create and sell their own digital products and tools with the objective of generating a new stream of income and to stop trading time for money.

Get free access to my Microproduct Masterclass, where I share how creating and selling small, fast-to-produce, and easy-to-sell digital products helped me build a multi six-figure business. Get your free access here: https://www.microproductlab.com/masterclass

# Franchising

### MEGAN REILLY

Befor skipping this chapter because franchising seems like it's complicated and complex, let me tell you this: I first learned about franchising by reading, *Franchise Management for Dummies*.

I knew nothing, I mean absolutely nothing, about franchising and today am COO and co-owner of an international franchise brand, Tippi Toes—a children's dance franchise.

Franchising is a phenomenal way to scale a business, and it is *not* just for those with a ton of business experience or an MBA. Anyone with a great and proven business concept, especially in service of something, can build a thriving franchise business.

Franchising is creating a set of processes that work well as a business and can be repeated by other people in different places. It is like copying and pasting a business and every process within the business. A franchisor is the person/team who creates the original business and offers the proven systems to others. A franchisee is the person/team who chooses to buy a franchise from a franchisor and execute the plan created by a franchisor.

Why franchise a business?

Who should franchise their business?

How would one franchise a business?

And why would someone buy a franchise?

Let's get into each one of these questions.

## WHY FRANCHISE A BUSINESS?

Franchising a business is a great way to scale and grow. You can expand your brand's reach, operate in new territories, provide opportunities for business owners, and serve more customers.

In the long term, it creates a system that affords the franchisor to continue to serve, grow, and generate revenue without being required to work the front lines every day. A franchisor goes from creating the brand and systems, to perfecting them over time, to fine-tuning and upkeep while all business metrics grow.

## WHO SHOULD FRANCHISE?

- Someone with a desire to expand a business.

- Someone who has a well-operating business.

- Someone who wants to grow but does not want to be involved in the front-line work forever.

- Someone who is willing to pass along her business experience to benefit others.

- Someone who has willingness for some risk.

- Someone who is willing to make changes, listen, and grow.

Please note, that list does *not* say:

- Someone with extensive business experience

- Someone with franchise experience

- Someone with tons of money

- Someone with high-power connections

Franchising is a wonderful solution for the right people. I have found it to be a joyful journey and I encourage others to explore it if that top list describes you!

## HOW TO FRANCHISE A BUSINESS?

Here is a high-level list of how to franchise from start to scale.

1. Start with a healthy business foundation.

2. Document everything.

3. Work with a franchise consultant, expert, or another franchisor for high level guidance.

4. Find a franchise specific attorney who you like—you will work with them a lot.

5. Choose franchise owners carefully.

6. Uphold brand standards within the system.

7. Be a partner for the franchisees.

## HEALTHY BUSINESS FOUNDATION

The most important piece to the puzzle is a healthy foundation of the business. Franchising should be considered only once a business and the processes have been tested, enhanced, and proven.

There is certainly a camp of people that may believe jumping into franchising before testing the business in real-time, but I disagree. There are valuable lessons that will be learned on the go, and it is worth spending a year or maybe two on the business before franchising.

We offered Tippi Toes dance classes for ten years before we began franchising. In our case, we never even considered franchising until 2007 and then we spent a year preparing and learning before selling our first franchise in 2009.

Franchising multiplies a business, so the original business should be profitable and running well. If the foundation is weak or broken and a company then begins franchising, those weaknesses will multiply, and the road becomes challenging and sometimes impossible. By spending time operating the business and planning for franchising, you equip yourself to fix any issues and plan ahead for the purpose of franchising.

So, you have a strong foundation and have proven your processes and now want to franchise. What do you do next? Start documenting!

## DOCUMENTING

The goal of franchising is that someone can purchase your franchise and execute the business just as you did. It is a turnkey concept, which means the systems and processes need to be thorough, clear, and tested.

I spent months documenting every single thing we did day in and day out. As I was running the day-to-day operations of a Tippi Toes location, I was simultaneously taking notes that would ultimately become our franchise manual.

You cannot document too much at this phase. Just write! Document! Be specific! Over time you will edit, revisit, and adjust, but when starting the documenting process just get it all out of your mind and onto paper.

There will be pages of information that will become directions for new franchise owners. They will become the map to building a business and the keys to a franchisee's success.

Spoiler alert—the processes continue to change forever! As the world changes, so do businesses, so be open to continual growth and making edits on the documents you create. Over time, the changes will become minimal, but the mindset of continual evolution is important for the franchisor to hold close.

### EXPERTS
The concept of franchising is basic, but the practice of franchising has many facets. Spend time with those who are in the franchising world and who are well-respected. Plan on eventually paying someone to work with you, but during the early stages, do everything you can to learn about the franchising community.

### FRANCHISE ATTORNEY
Is a specific franchise attorney necessary? Yes. One hundred percent yes! Do not shortcut this step. Interview attorneys because you will work closely with them in the development of your franchise business.

If we go too much further, we will find ourselves in the weeds, so let's leave it at this. If you want to have success as a franchisor, align yourself with an excellent franchise attorney and the benefit will far outweigh the expense.

### CHOOSE WISELY
Once you have prepared and are ready to award franchises to people, choose wisely. Many brands choose growth over

everything and do not care if a franchisee aligns well with the brand. I will never understand that approach.

Appointing franchisees who are great matches for the brand and franchise strengthens the entire ecosystem.

It is faster growth for the franchisor to sell a bunch of franchises and not worry about alignment, however, brands that explode on the scene and appoint a franchise to anyone with the capital often find themselves doing clean-up duty six, twelve, or eighteen months later.

While every franchise owner will not have a fairytale ending, it is key to appoint a franchise to someone who gives you all green lights and no red flags. Slow and healthy growth is far superior to faster and sloppy growth, especially in the franchise world.

## UPHOLD BRAND STANDARDS

Franchise owners look for brand standards and guidelines from the franchisor. A franchisor must be clear with the standards and guides. A franchisor should also be prepared to adjust standards as the company evolves.

When franchise owners break out of the framework, the franchisor owes it to the company and every other franchise owner to uphold the expectations all franchise owners agreed to when they signed the agreement.

A franchisee may violate standards for a variety of reasons, and many of those reasons are in good faith and not out of irreverence. A franchisor should respond quickly, clearly, and kindly so expectations are clear for franchise owners.

A franchise that is sloppy with standards will become sloppy in operations and could ultimately lead to a failed franchise.

## *BE A PARTNER*

A franchise system grows when a group of people come together. While the franchisor does develop the concept and processes, and drives the overall business, franchisees bring a powerful dynamic to the brand. Franchisors with an open-door policy open themselves to creativity from those executing the business every day.

As a franchisor, I am always open to the ideas and feedback from franchise owners, and their opinions are key to our development. Not every idea is implemented, but every idea is heard, considered, and appreciated. As they say, two minds are better than one!

Franchisees' success is our main objective as the franchisor. This is why we approach our franchise owners with a partner mentality. A franchisor should want the very best for every franchisee.

## WHY WOULD SOMEONE BUY A FRANCHISE?

To make an impact with a proven method.

To build a business with support.

To diversify investments.

To be a part of a system, but also to be your own boss.

To avoid a large portion of the typical pitfalls of business ownership.

To be a part of a community with similar goals.

## *SEASONED BUSINESSPERSON*

Those who come into franchising with business experience often use franchising as an investment tool. Or sometimes they see a lucrative model and snatch up the opportunity.

## NEW BUSINESS OWNER

Novice business owners see franchising as a way to learn about operating and owning a business without doing so on a deserted island. It is a way to learn with a sort of safety net compared to starting something from scratch and alone.

## PASSIONATE BUSINESS OWNER

Some come into a franchise system as a believer of the brand and mission. Their desire to be a part of the brand and impact drives them every step of the way.

Franchising is a brilliant concept that offers growth for all involved across a multitude of industries. While I started out as a "dummie", I have become an expert through years of trial and error. We are all capable of learning new things and I believe books like this help us recognize our potential in all different areas of our lives!

Megan Reilly is the COO and co-owner of Tippi Toes®, an international franchisor of children's dance. For more than a decade, Megan has helped franchise owners build and grow their own businesses around the world.

A 2012 Shark Tank alum, Megan and her business partner were awarded a deal by Mark Cuban, yet decided to grow their business on their own and have since reached thirty-five franchises and published children's music that reached number one on iTunes.

Megan is the creator and host of one of the Top 12 Parenting Podcasts on Apple Podcasts, Who Is Your Momma Podcast, where she speaks to the mothers of some of the world's most successful, CEOs, athletes, and entertainers.

Megan also works as an expert mentor for Jesse Itzler's elite coaching program, Elite365.

Megan and her husband, Chris, have been married since 2007 and have three daughters who are six, eight, and ten.

This is a self-discovery worksheet to determine your path. Great ideas begin with reflections and direction. There are two sections—one for those who want to franchise and the second is for those who want to purchase a franchise.
https://thepublishingcircle.com/franchise

# Please Leave A Review

Thank you for purchasing this book. Doing so makes you a part of raising funds to help feed the hungry.

Would you take one more step to help keep this book visible? Leaving a review is the way to help further. Of course, we'd love it if you share about the book with your fellow entrepreneurs!

You can leave a review at your favorite site by going here: https://books2read.com/BizWomen

And remember:

*In all you do, BE the blessing.*
LINDA STIRLING

Printed in Great Britain
by Amazon

44031142R00155